IRIAF 2010 – The Modern Iranian Air Force
Tom Cooper, Babak Taghvaee and Liam F. Devlin

IRIAF 2010

The
Modern
Iranian
Air
Force

Tom Cooper, Babak Taghvaee and Liam F. Devlin

HARPIA
PUBLISHING+

Copyright © 2010 Harpia Publishing, L.L.C. & Moran Publishing, L.L.C. Joint Venture
2803 Sackett Street, Houston, TX 77098-1125, U.S.A.
iriaf2010@harpia-publishing.com

All rights reserved.

No part of this publication may be copied, reproduced, stored electronically or transmitted
in any manner or in any form whatsoever without the written permission of the publisher.

Consulting and inspiration by Kerstin Berger
Drawings by Ugo Crisponi and Tom Cooper
Map by Mark Lepko
Editorial by Thomas Newdick
Layout by Norbert Novak, www.media-n.at, Vienna

Printed at Grasl Druck & Neue Medien, Austria

ISBN 978-0-9825539-3-0

Harpia Publishing, L.L.C. is a member of

Contents

Introduction 7

Abbreviations 9

A short history of the Iranian Air Force 11

The IRIAF in 2010 15

Tactical Fighter Base 1   Mehrabad 17

Tactical Fighter Base 2   Tabriz 55

Tactical Fighter Base 3   Nojeh 67

Tactical Fighter Base 4   Vahdati 73

Tactical Fighter Base 5   Ardestani 81

Tactical Fighter Base 6   Yassini 85

Tactical Fighter Base 7   Dowran 93

Tactical Fighter Base 8   Baba'i 111

Tactical Fighter Base 9   Bandar Abbas 137

Tactical Fighter Base 10   Konarak 141

Tactical Fighter Base 14   Imam Reza 145

Other IRIAF bases 149

Order of Battle 153

Map of Iran 158

Introduction

Iran is a country equivalent in size to Germany, France, Spain, Portugal, the Netherlands and Belgium combined. It is situated in the middle of one of the strategically most important regions of the world, an area that holds around 70 per cent of global hydrocarbon resources. Iran is also the inheritor of thousands of years of military tradition. These factors not only put the country in the centre stage of world events, but also strongly influenced the evolution of its air force over the past 85 years.

The purpose of this book is to provide a single point of reference and a simple-to-use summary of the development of the Iranian air arm and its bases, and the current state of the Islamic Republic of Iran Air Force (IRIAF). Despite its illustrious past, today's Iranian Air Force is no longer the prime factor behind Iran's status as a major regional power. However, the IRIAF continues to proudly serve its nation. Even among today's most advanced air forces, it would be hard to find parallels to the dedication of IRIAF officers, airmen, pilots and groundcrew to their nation and their duty. These qualities are without doubt one of the 'secrets' behind the air arm's survival against all odds in the past three decades.

In addition to conducting new research for this book, the authors also called upon their extensive series of publications – including three books and more than three dozen articles – on the Iranian military, its technological elements, equipment and history. These books and articles were published in the last decade in the UK, US and elsewhere, and were mainly based on interviews with participants, as well as corroborated news reports emerging from Iran.

While refraining from offering any political analysis or judgements (which can be found in abundance in the media in recent times), the authors have preferred to concentrate on the topic at hand. The contemporary Iranian Air Force has long been an interesting and exotic topic of discussion. Unfortunately, it has also been a subject frequently tainted by misinformation, guesswork, and not a little prejudice. The authors' hope is that this reference work will provide both enthusiasts and professional observers with an accurate portrait of the Iranian Air Force in 2010.

Tom Cooper, Babak Taghvaee and Liam F. Devlin,
July 2010

Abbreviations

AB	Air Base
AB/AS	Agusta-Bell/Agusta-Sikorsky (Italian helicopter manufacturer)
AEW&C	airborne early warning and control
ASW	anti-submarine warfare
Brig Gen	brigadier general
C4I	command, control, communications, computers and intelligence
CAP	combat air patrol
CBU	Cluster Bomb Unit
CIA	Central Intelligence Agency
C-in-C	commander in chief
COIN	counter-insurgent or counter-insurgency
CRC	control and reporting centre
CSAR	combat search and rescue
ECM	electronic countermeasures
ELINT	electronic intelligence
FOD	foreign object damage
FS	Fighter Squadron
Gen	general (military commissioned officer rank)
GP	general-purpose (bomb)
HESA	Farsi abbreviation for Iran Aircraft Manufacturing Industrial Company, sometimes shortened in English to IAMIC or IAMI
IACI	Iran Aircraft Industries
IAMI	Iranian Aircraft Manufacturing Industries (Hessa in Persian)
ICBM	intercontinental ballistic missile
IFF/SIF	identification, friend or foe/selective identification feature
IIAA	Imperial Iranian Army Aviation (official designation until 1979)
IIAF	Imperial Iranian Air Force (official designation from 1924 until 1979)
IINA	Imperial Iranian Naval Aviation (official designation until 1979)
IR	infra-red; electromagnetic radiation with wavelength longer than deepest red light sensed as heat
IRGC	Islamic Revolutionary Guards Corps (Iranian militia originally organised in support of the newly emerging Islamic government of Iran; popularly known as 'Pasdaran', but also includes the Basij militia)
IRIAA	Islamic Republic of Iran Army Aviation (official designation since 1979)
IRIAF	Islamic Republic of Iran Air Force (official designation since 1979)
IRINA	Islamic Republic of Iran Naval Aviation (official designation since 1979)
KIA	killed in action
km	kilometre
LGB	laser-guided bomb
Lt Col	lieutenant colonel (military commissioned officer rank)
Maj	major (military commissioned officer rank)
Maj Gen	major general (military commissioned officer rank)
MANPADS	man-portable air defence system (light surface-to-air missiles that can be carried and deployed in combat by a single soldier)
MAP	Military Assistance Program
MiG	Mikoyan i Gurevich (the design bureau)
NCO	non-commissioned officer
NSA	National Security Agency
PGM	precision-guided munition (guided bombs and air-to-surface missiles)
SAM	surface-to-air missile
SAR	search and rescue
SAVAK	Saseman Amniat va Etelaot Keshwar, or Organisation for Information and Protection of the Country, Iranian equivalent to the CIA and NSA
SIGINT	signals intelligence
SSJD	Self-Sufficiency Jihad Directorate
TAB	Tactical Air Base
TAS	Transport Aircraft Squadron
TFB	Tactical Fighter Base
TFS	Tactical Fighter Squadron
TWA	Trans World Airlines
USD	US Dollar

A short history of the Iranian Air Force

A rich heritage

It was in the early 1920s that the then de facto ruler of Iran, Reza Khan, recognised the advantages of developing an effective air power and air communications system. Iran was a large country with under-developed rail and road networks. Correspondingly, in 1922, Reza Khan established an Air Office within the Iranian Army Headquarters, to assess the possibility of establishing a military air arm. At this time, the Junkers concern had established a branch in Iran and was operating postal and passenger services between Tehran, Bandar Pahlavi, Mashhad and Shiraz. Naturally, the Iranian Army's first aircraft became a Junkers F 13 transport flown by a German pilot and based at Ghaleh-Morghi airfield, outside Tehran. In 1923, an Aero A.30 army cooperation biplane was purchased from subscriptions raised by the Gilan Brigade and the Astarabad Brigade (the subsequent Gorgan Brigade). At the same time, the first military flying facilities (a hangar constructed of matting and a tent) were erected at Ghaleh-Morghi.

By early 1924, the Iranian Army possessed a miscellany of reconnaissance-bombers purchased from the Soviet Union, and four transport aircraft obtained from Germany. A number of Iranian officers had been sent to France and Russia for pilot training, and a small batch of reconnaissance biplanes was acquired from the Soviet Union. A number of different aircraft were ordered from France, although only one managed to reach its final destination, on 1 June 1924 (11 Khordad 1303 in the Persian Calendar, celebrated as Air Force Day until 1979). By then, an Army cooperation unit had been established at Ghaleh-Morghi. With the help of French, German and Russian advisers, local facilities for pilot training were created at Mehrabad and the Shahbaz aircraft factory was established at Dowshan Tappeh. Fleet airworthiness gradually improved, enabling the fledgling air arm to make use of its available aircraft against tribal insurgents, as well as for observation and liaison purposes.

In 1932 the Joint Military Aviation Office of the Imperial Iranian Armed Forces was reorganised as the Imperial Iranian Air Force (IIAF). At the same time, a major modernisation programme was instituted, in the course of which a number of Royal Swedish Air Force personnel were contracted to act as instructors for Iranian pilots, who were trained on 18 de Havilland Tiger Moths purchased from the UK. From then until 1948, all flying personnel were trained in Iran. During the 1930s, the IIAF considerably increased the number of personnel and flying hours, as additional aircraft were purchased from abroad. Work also continued to improve training, organisation and technical infrastructure. On 23 September 1933 a training school for observers was established, followed by a Technical School for mechanics. On 22 March 1936 the state-owned Shahbaz Works was established at Dowshan Tappeh as the first aircraft assembly factory in the Middle East.

Meanwhile, between 1933 and 1935, the IIAF had further expanded its fleet of light bombers and army cooperation biplanes, eventually establishing four air regiments. The 1st Air Regiment, based at Ghaleh-Morghi, comprised one fighter squadron and two light bomber squadrons, while the 2nd, 3rd and 4th Air Regiments each possessed one squadron of army cooperation aircraft and were based at Tabriz, Mashhad and Ahwaz, respectively.

As of 1940 the IIAF inventory amounted to no less than 215 aircraft, and continued its growth towards a planned strength of 300 combat fighters and bombers within five regiments. However, in an operational sense the IIAF was still tied to the Army. Although the pilot schools' output increased significantly, new pilots and other crews lacked realistic combat training, and an efficient maintenance organisation was not yet in place. World War II, and the occupation of Iran by British, US and Soviet forces that began on 25 August 1941, interrupted the IIAF's expansion programme and left it inactive, its personnel demoralised. At this time the

IIAF operated 283 aircraft and was organised into 11 wings and 24 squadrons at five airfields. Nevertheless, foreign powers had little faith in Iran. Any indigenous efforts to keep the IIAF operational during the occupation were viewed as a 'rather ineffective, Persian way' of doing business. As of 1945, the British were convinced that the future of the Iranian Air Force was very bleak.

Nevertheless, the IIAF survived this difficult period. Following the withdrawal of occupying forces, the new sovereign of Iran, Mohamad Reza Shah-e Pahlavi, personally oversaw improvements made to the air force, including the addition of a regiment of British-made Hawker Hurricane fighters. Much more than the British, however, it was the Americans who subsequently took over the role of supporting the service, initially through the provision of loans and technical assistance.

On 1 May 1948 the first group of IIAF officers and non-commissioned officers left Iran for the US to begin training under the Military Assistance Program (MAP), which saw Iran take delivery of a considerable number of surplus US military aircraft, including Republic P-47D Thunderbolt fighter-bombers, Douglas C-47 transports, Piper L-4 air observation aircraft, Boeing-Stearman PT-13 Kaydet primary trainers, and North American AT-6 basic trainers. These aircraft were provided almost free of charge, Iran only having to pay for the training and the spare parts support, using a credit that was offered to Iran under very favourable terms.

Several months later, on 23 September 1948, the first apprentice technician courses began in Iran. The acquisition of new aircraft and the training of new personnel were accompanied by a major reorganisation and expansion of the IIAF. Although the air arm still remained under the operational control of the Army General Staff, it soon possessed over 300 tactical aircraft organised within seven fighter and fighter-bomber squadrons, six reconnaissance squadrons, a transport unit, liaison flights, an overhaul and maintenance plant, and various training establishments. The latter training facilities included an Air Officers' Training College providing a three-year course for pilots and navigators, an Engineer Officers' Training College, an Advanced Officers' Training College and an NCO Technical Training School.

During the early 1950s, 14 Iranian pilots selected for training on jet fighters travelled to Germany, where they flew Lockheed T-33A jet trainers and Republic F-84G Thunderjet fighter-bombers under the auspices of a US Military Assistance Advisory Group. Iran later received its own T-33A jets beginning in May 1956, and specialised jet training courses were subsequently undertaken under the supervision of the USAF instructors.

By the mid-1950s the IIAF comprised seven wings with 185 aircraft deployed on six bases. Major units comprised one wing flying F-84G and P-47D fighter-bombers from Ahvaz, Esfahan, Mashhad, Tehran and Shiraz; an air depot wing at Dowshan Tappeh; and air transport and training wings at Ghaleh-Morghi.

The primary concern of the air arm at this time remained internal security, and its operational strength remained relatively low. The situation began to change during the late 1950s, as Iranian military commanders gradually began to appreciate the importance of an effective air arm for both defence and transport purposes.

In 1955 the IIAF finally became a separate arm within the structure of the Imperial Iranian Armed Services (IIAS). At the same time it began to develop in terms of strength and efficiency, with financial, technical and training assistance provided by the MAP. The situation changed entirely once the charismatic and well-connected Brig Gen Mohamad A. Khatami was appointed the C-in-C of the IIAF, at the age of 38. An excellent fighter pilot and a dedicated and forceful commander, Khatami contributed significantly to the subsequent development of the service.

During the mid-1960s the IIAF received two squadrons of modern Northrop F-5A/B Freedom Fighter lightweight fighters provided through MAP channels. Iran then began ordering from the US additional F-5s and – more importantly – the advanced and highly capable McDonnell Douglas F-4 Phantom II fighter.

By the early 1970s the US and UK also provided Iran with the basic elements of an early warning radar network and advanced air defence systems, which eventually provided good coverage of Iran's long borders.

A short history of the Iranian Air Force

In subsequent years the IIAF experienced an unprecedented period of growth and a very rapid build-up of forces. Three successive orders for over 140 F-4E Phantom IIs, issued in 1971, 1972 and 1973, attracted worldwide attention, and the IIAF soon became financially and technically involved in research and development projects related to a number of very advanced weapon systems. Through the acquisition of hundreds of other advanced fighters, transports, reconnaissance and intelligence-gathering aircraft, helicopters and 'smart' weapons throughout the mid-1970s, the IIAF completed its transition from 'infant' air am of the 1920s, to the 'unenthusiastic' and critically under-funded service of the 1930s and 1940s, via the 'advanced flying club' of the 1950s, to emerge as one of the world's 10 leading air arms in the late 1970s. Although this massive build-up threatened to overstretch the available national resources, and involved the massive presence of foreign advisory teams in Iran, the development of local training and support infrastructure was well under way by the late 1970s. With suitable leadership, these foundations promised the IIAF a long-term future independent of direct foreign involvement.

In light of serious doubts raised by Western observers over Iran's ability to embark on prolonged military operations, the air arm was designed and developed to ensure it could inflict severe, Blitzkrieg-style pre-emptive blows against potential aggressors. The main concerns over the viability of prolonged operations were the questionable serviceability of equipment and logistics, a shortage of experienced manpower and a lack of initiative. The new-look air arm was even fancied to temporarily stop a Soviet invasion, supporting ground units with both firepower and logistics until US help could arrive. By 1979 the IIAF had therefore become the Iran's 'first line of defence', with its morale and readiness rates reaching unprecedented levels.

The Revolution of 1979, however, and the turmoil that followed, left the Iranian Air Force under a heavy strain. Political divisions within its ranks, and involvement in various forms of protests and coup attempts resulted in the new government purging a sizeable number of the service's personnel with questionable allegiance. At the same time, a significant part of its capability was demobilised. Another shock was to follow in late September 1980, when the air arm – now renamed as the Islamic Republic of Iran Air Force (IRIAF) – found itself on the receiving end of an all-out Iraqi invasion. It was this attack, in combination with international sanctions, which provided the sternest test for the IRIAF. Although practically grounded by that time, the air force quickly regrouped and responded to the Iraqi invasion within only a few hours. Furthermore, in accordance with plans outlined years before, the next day – 23 September – the IRIAF launched Operation Kaman-99 into the skies of Iraq. Employing more than 140 combat aircraft, Iran attacked Iraqi military targets, throwing the enemy air force off balance and forcing it onto the defensive.

Subsequently, the IRIAF launched a major – and again pre-planned – counter-value campaign against Iraq's economic targets. Attacks by the F-4 Phantom fighter-bombers of the IRIAF against targets in the Baghdad area flown during October and November 1980 became so regular and famous that they were nick-named 'Baghdad Express'. Simultaneously, the IRIAF brought the Iraqi oil industry to its knees through a series of such severe blows that Iraq was forced to stop exporting and start importing petrochemical products.

This gradually gave way to a campaign that concentrated on supporting Iranian ground troops fighting the Iraqi invaders in the province of Khuzestan. Despite demonstrating varying levels of competence and initiative, as well as sustaining significant losses, the Iranian Air Force played a crucial role in the first few months of the war, holding back the Iraqi advance until Iranian ground forces were mobilised and deployed in sufficient numbers along the front lines. The IRIAF units equipped with transport aircraft and helicopters played a crucial role in transporting reinforcements and equipment from all parts of the country to the front lines of the war with Iraq.

In the subsequent years the IRIAF fought a massive and prolonged battle for air superiority over Khuzestan. In dozens of complex air battles that raged through 1981, 1982 and 1983, the Iranian F-4 Phantom and F-14 Tomcat interceptors caused heavy losses to the fighter-bombers and interceptors of the Iraqi Air Force. Simultaneously, the Iranian F-4 Phantom and F-5 Tiger fighter-bombers hit the Iraqi ground forces heavily, several times causing entire brigades of the Iraqi Army to collapse and thus playing a crucial role in the lift of the siege of Abadan, and the liberation of Khorramshahr and other towns in western Khuzestan, which had been completely devastated by the Iraqis.

With extensive financial help from abroad, particularly from Kuwait and Saudi Arabia, the Iraqis then began introducing ever more advanced interceptor aircraft of French and Soviet origin. Ironically, while convincing not only themselves, but also most Western observers that the IRIAF was all but 'dead', they began developing one of most sophisticated and complex air defence systems worldwide. Realising that the conflict with Iraq had developed into a form of attrition war, by mid-1983 the IRIAF began concentrating on conserving its remaining assets and gave up fighting the battle for air superiority over Khuzestan. The force was not defeated but after providing a crucial contribution to the liberation of western Khuzestan and other parts of Iran along the border to Iraq, it concentrated on protecting the skies over strategically important installations, such as the oil exporting terminal on Khark Island, as well as major cities, foremost Teheran and Esfahan.

Later on, the IRIAF found itself involved in equally protracted and bitter maritime and interdiction campaigns, as well as a campaign of targeting counter-value assets. Over the time, such selective deployment of air power eventually developed into the so-called 'Tanker War' and the 'War of the Cities', forcing the Iranian air force to continuously develop new tactics and techniques. In the course of these campaigns, the IRIAF excelled in flying highly complex operations including multiple in-flight refuelling operations at low level in order to hit targets deep inside Iraq. One of best known such operations was the famous 'H-3 Blitz' raid, flown by a formation of F-4 Phantoms supported by two tanker aircraft against the H-3 air base complex in western Iraq, in April 1981.

The IRIAF also maintained pressure upon the Iraqi oil export industry by repeatedly targeting of all major refineries and pumping stations along various oil pipelines. Attacks against such installations were flown until the last days of the war. Through all of this conflict, the air force's units equipped with reconnaissance platforms, foremost those flying RF-4 and RF-5 fighters, continued providing crucially important intelligence, while transport units provided all sorts of support in a massive and continuous effort to quickly shift ground units, reinforcements, equipment and supplies from various parts of Iran to the front lines, as well as evacuate casualties to the hospitals in major cities.

Nevertheless, the longest conventional war of the 20th century was a double-edged sword: it not only proved a unique source of combat experience, but also consumed a significant portion of the highly trained and motivated IRIAF flight crews, and their equipment. Correspondingly, the air force began putting emphasis on training of new flight- and ground crews, on improving the maintenance of aircraft and the development of new weapons.

While fighting the imposed war against Iraq, the IRIAF faced an unprecedented challenge from the Iraqi Air Force and air defences, which enjoyed far less problematic access to modern equipment, spares and replacement aircraft. This disadvantage forced Iran to formulate unique solutions to its various problems.

Self-sufficiency suddenly became the motto of the day, especially within the air force. The service adapted surprisingly quickly to this challenge and the war left the IRIAF with a previously almost unimaginable pool of experience and knowledge. The IRIAF has called upon these resources not only to help keep its equipment operational during the war with Iraq but also ever since.

The IRIAF in 2010

The years since the end of the war with Iraq, and in particular recent events, have proven that Iran can hold its ground and maintain its independence from foreign influence amid continuing Western sanctions and pressure, as well as mismanagement on the domestic side.

Iran's modern-day military strategy against foreign threats is designed primarily to defend the Islamic Republic through deterrence, but also through retaliation, if necessary. Although the IRIAF's offensive capabilities are usually downplayed, the air force still provides the backbone of the nation's air defences, and operates some of its most capable offensive platforms. Furthermore, although the ability of the air force to project power much beyond Iranian borders – particularly against Israel or Saudi Arabia – is often questioned, there is no doubt that this force is capable of deterring or defending against most conventional threats posed by Iran's neighbours. The air force is also equipped to exercise effective control over most of the Persian Gulf, the Strait of Hormuz, as well as large parts of the Gulf of Oman. Under the given circumstances, and also in the face of future challenges, the IRIAF remains a force to be reckoned with.

While an air defence force was created through the separation of the IRIAF's ground-based air defence elements in late 2008, the air force remains a significant military power. IRIAF strength is estimated at around 52,000 personnel, deployed at 10 major bases. The IRIAF currently operates a total of 20 fighter and fighter-bomber squadrons, a single reconnaissance squadron, and around a dozen tanker, transport and search and rescue (SAR) units.

The air force remains largely dependent on vintage US-made aircraft, foremost the Grumman F-14A Tomcat, McDonnell Douglas F-4 Phantom II, and Northrop F-5E Tiger II, almost 200 of which are kept in various levels of operational condition. In addition, the IRIAF operates small fleets of Russian-made fighters, including the Mikoyan i Gurevich MiG-29 and Sukhoi Su-24MK, as well as Chinese-made Chengdu F-7N/FT-7 point-defence fighters.

Although no new aircraft have been procured from abroad for almost 15 years, Iran is working on the development of indigenous combat aircraft, including advanced stealth capabilities. Iran has also modified its existing aircraft, resulting in the Saegheh (Lightning) fighter jet, which represents a modification of the F-5E. At least as important is the fact that the IRIAF is increasingly making use of unmanned aerial vehicles (UAVs). Two families of reconnaissance, targeting and attack UAVs have been developed, and two additional families are under development. Although details remain scarce, four major air bases are known to operate squadrons of indigenous Mohajer-4 and Ababil-3 UAVs. There are plans to expand the UAV force so that each air base will be equipped with at least a squadron of such aircraft, and also to field a fleet of unmanned combat aerial vehicles (UCAVs). Iran was a pioneer of the combat deployment of UCAVs, arming its UAVs and deploying them in combat as early as 1986.

IRIAF planners well understand the value of airborne early warning and C4I systems, airborne intelligence, electronic warfare platforms, advanced precision-guided munitions (PGMs), UAVs and aerial refuelling. The air force has experienced significant progress in the arena of C4I, but its development of an airborne early warning and control (AEW&C) system likely suffered when the sole available platform crashed in September 2009. The aircraft, an Ilyushin Il-76 Adnan modified by Iraq in the 1980s through the addition of a large rotodome on top of its rear fuselage crashed during a parade, killing all seven on board, including the two leading officers of the project.

IRIAF training coupled with the entire defensive doctrine of delay and attrition indicate that the main purpose of the air force today is to slow an invasion. In this manner, the IRIAF would focus on causing attrition, buying time for other elements of the Iranian military to deploy to the field, until a rapid diplomatic solution to the hostilities can be found. Furthermore, due to its extensive transport capability, the IRIAF continues to play a prominent role during natural disasters and whenever there is a requirement for the swift transfer of troops and equipment from one part of the country to another.

Prior to 1979, Iran had no air academy, and most of its pilots were trained outside the country, primarily in the US, but also in the UK, West Germany, Pakistan and even Israel. Since 1986, new generations of IRIAF fighter pilots have been exclusively trained at a new Air Force Academy in Iran. Before being selected for flight training, prospective students are first screened for their ideological conformity, and are then put through similar aptitude tests as found in most other air forces around the world. Ground training takes place at both Tehran and Esfahan, and basic flight training is undertaken at Kushk-e Nosrat airfield near Tehran. Basic jet training is conducted at Esfahan, where students fly the F-5A/B, Simorgh and FT-7 aircraft under the supervision of experienced instructors.

Connected to the role of the Air Force Academy has been the work on local assembly of training aircraft of US, Swiss and domestic origins. At the same time, ever more ambitious projects have been directed towards the reverse engineering of various spare parts, including engine components. Iran has also made significant strides in the field of composite materials. Together, these efforts have resulted in the development of a capability to locally manufacture subassemblies for aircraft structures, as well as electronic components. In spite of many setbacks and serious problems in organising and financing indigenous programmes, Iran is well on the road to self-sufficiency. Over time, Iranian Aircraft Industries (IACI) has begun work on a number of indigenous aircraft projects. The organisation presides over a number of large factories and aircraft-overhaul facilities that were originally established in the 1970s with US support. It is also responsible for several technical universities and research institutes, and a number of private enterprises. However, although a few of these indigenous projects have reached the prototype stage, none has so far entered series production. It remains to be seen if any of the related projects will receive the necessary funding, since the government has been prioritising other projects, mainly related to surface-to-surface missiles. It is mainly for this reason that, despite the availability of domestic know-how, the IRIAF still faces spare-parts shortages, and in many cases still depends on foreign sources.

A number of important acquisition decisions will soon need to be made regarding future combat, training and transport types. However, long-term replacement projects for those airframes reaching or surpassing their intended service life are currently effectively on hold. In the meantime, the IRIAF is in urgent need of complex spare parts for its combat, transport and other types of aircraft and helicopters. Nevertheless, the Iranian air force continues to soldier on and serve with the assets it has to hand.

Tactical Fighter Base 1 Mehrabad

In 1938 a new airfield was constructed near the village of Mehrabad, to the west of Tehran, which was then still outside the city. The airfield became a base for the IIAF Flying School, equipped with 20 aircraft. During World War II, Ghaleh-Morghi was controlled by the Soviets, while Mehrabad was under the control of British forces. In October 1945, following the end of the war, Mehrabad was returned to the IIAF. In 1949 the airfield became the first Iranian base for US-made aircraft, when the first out of more than 60 P-47 Thunderbolts eventually made available to Iran were based there.

Eight years later, the IIAF's 1st and 3rd Fighter Squadrons, then flying F-84G Thunderjet fighters, moved from Ghaleh-Morghi and Mehrabad airfield was officially declared as the 1st Tactical Fighter Base (TFB.1). Finally, in 1960, all the Thunderjets and Thunderbolts were replaced by North American F-86F Sabres, the number of which grew to such a level that a third squadron was established with the type. Additionally, the sole reconnaissance unit of the IIAF, the 11th Tactical Reconnaissance Squadron, flew 12 RT-33A reconnaissance jets from the base.

On 12 January 1965 the IIAF received its first batch of F-5A Freedom Fighters through MAP channels. On their service entry with the 1st FS, this unit was re-designated as the 101st TFS. Within the following two years, all the remaining Sabres were replaced by F-5A/Bs, and TFB.1 thus became the home of the 101st, 102nd and 103rd Tactical Fighter Squadrons. Similarly, the 11th TRS was re-equipped with 12 RF-5A Freedom Fighters in 1968, by which time Mehrabad AB had expanded to become the largest Iranian transport base.

The first transport aircraft stationed at TFB.1 were C-47 transports, acquired in the early 1950s and operated by two squadrons throughout most of the 1960s. Additionally, TFB.1 also became home to a sole Light Transport Squadron, a VIP Transport Squadron, and its own SAR Flight.

Through the 1970s, TFB.1 became the biggest and most modern air base in the entire Middle East, and was home to units possessing a wide variety of equipment and capabilities. All the F-5As were swiftly replaced with F-4Es, even though the number of operational fighter units decreased to two. On the other hand, Mehrabad remained the home

Table 1: IIAF units based at TFB.1, 1978

Unit designation	Aircraft type	Remarks
11th TFS	16 x F-4E/D	Also acting as Fighter Weapons School/ Combat Commanders' School
12th TFS	16 x F-4E	
11th TRS	6 x RF-4C/E, 10 x RF-5A	
12th TRS	4 x RC-130H, 2 x Boeing 707-3J9C	Aircraft equipped for SIGINT and ELINT gathering, respectively
11th TAS	12 x C-130E/H	
12th TAS	12 x C-130E/H	
Tanker/Transport Squadron	14 x Boeing 707-3J9C, 7 x Boeing 747-131ST, 4 x Boeing 747-2J9F	
Light Transport Squadron	18 x Fokker F27-400M and F27-600	
Falcon Star Squadron	2 x L-1329 JetStar, 3 x Falcon 20F	
VIP Transport Squadron	1 x Boeing 707, 2 x AB.212	
11th Helicopter Transport Squadron	5 x CH-47C	
SAR Squadron	9 x AB.205 and Bell 214C	

of the surviving RF-5As, which were now operated by the 11th TRS together with the RF-4 – the latter a specially equipped reconnaissance variant of the Phantom II. TFB.1 also became the main hub of all IIAF reconnaissance, transport and tanker operations, as well as the home base of the leading training unit, the Combat Commanders' School (essentially similar to the USAF's Fighter Weapons School). TFB.1 remained the largest and most active Iranian Air Force base through the late 1970s, by which time several major maintenance facilities had been established there. With the primary task of protecting the capital of Iran, Mehrabad was by the late 1970s home base to the units in Table 1.

On the afternoon of 22 September 1988, TFB.1 found itself on the receiving end of a raid flown by three Iraqi Tupolev Tu-22B bombers. Although most of the Iraqi bombs failed to explode, they managed to fatally damage a Lockheed C-130 Hercules, a Boeing 707 and an F-4E on the ground. Despite the raid, the following morning no fewer than 40 F-4s were launched from Mehrabad to attack major Iraqi bases in the Baghdad area. Subsequently, Boeing 707 and 747 tankers from Mehrabad provided aerial refuelling support to fighters from this and other Iranian air bases throughout the war. Transport aircraft from Mehrabad-based units played perhaps an even more important function in hauling ground forces, their equipment and supplies from various parts of Iran to the battlefields.

Most of the locally based F-4Es were sent as replacements to other air bases, thereby reducing the number of operational fighter squadrons to a single unit. The last Phantoms left Mehrabad in 1990, when they were replaced by a dozen MiG-29s. Nevertheless, Mehrabad remains the home base for a number of other important units (Table 2).

11th Tactical Fighter Squadron

This unit inherits a proud tradition, extending back to the 1930s, when the 1st Squadron was established as part of the 1st Air Regiment, then based at Ghaleh-Morghi, and flying British-made Hawker Fury biplane fighters. In 1939 the 1st Squadron became the first and the only Iranian unit to be equipped with Hawker Hurricane fighters. It was reformed in 1943 as part of No. 1 Bomber Regiment and was equipped with several Avro Ansons. Re-equipped again, the same unit flew Hurricane Mk IIC fighter-bombers during 1945–47, when it was stationed at Ghaleh-Morghi. In 1949 the now 1st Squadron was re-equipped – this time with P-47D Thunderbolts – and moved to Mehrabad AB. Thunderbolts remained in service until 15 May 1957, when the unit was reorganised as the 1st Tactical Fighter Squadron, and was equipped with F-84Gs.

Another reorganisation and re-designation followed on 12 January 1965, when the 1st TFS became the 101st TFS, re-equipped with 11 F-5As and 3 F-5Bs. Northrop's lightweight fighters remained in service until 1971, when all gave way to the first of 32 F-4Es, ordered by Iran in 1969. From then onwards, the best-equipped and newest Phantoms

Table 2: IRIAF units based at TFB.1, 2010

Unit designation	Aircraft type	Remarks
11th TFS	MiG-29 and MiG-29UB	
12th TAS	C-130E/H	
Reconnaissance Squadron	RC-130H, Boeing 707-3J9C	Aircraft equipped for COMINT and SIGINT gathering, respectively
Tanker/Transport Squadron	Boeing 747-131F, Boeing 747-2J9F	
F27 Squadron	Fokker F27-400M/600	
Falcon Star Squadron	L-1329 JetStar and Falcon 20F	
VIP Transport Squadron	1 x Boeing 707-386C, 1 x Boeing 707-3J9C, 2 x Falcon 50EX, 2 x JetStar II, 3 x AB.212, 2 x Bell 412	
11th Helicopter Transport Squadron	CH-47C	
SAR Squadron	Bell 214C	

always served with this unit, which subsequently adopted the role of fighter weapons school, in the process becoming the IIAF's premier fighter asset.

Re-designated once again in early 1974, as the 11th TFS, the unit saw its first combat deployment in early 1975, during a series of border skirmishes with Iraq. In the course of this crisis, 12 F-4Es from the 11th and 12th TFS flew power-projection sorties along – and sometimes beyond – the border with Iraq. The offensively configured F-4s were armed with M117 GP bombs and LAU-61/A rocket pods, while four F-4Es were armed with AIM-7 Sparrow and AIM-9 Sidewinder air-to-air missiles.

Following the 1980 invasion of Iran, most of the F-4Es from the 11th and 12th TFS were assigned to other units, based on airfields closer to the battlefields. By the end of the war, only 10 Phantoms remained assigned to the 11th TFS, and the decision was made to re-equip this squadron with the first batch of MiG-29 fighters acquired from the then Soviet Union. The first MiG-29s began arriving in Iran in June 1990. Ever since, MiG-29s from Mehrabad have been assigned with the protection of the Iranian capital, as well as escorting VIP aircraft.

In addition, during the early 1990s, Shiraz air base sent its 71st TFS to TFB.1 to take part in the introduction of the Su-24MK to IRIAF service. This prompted the air force to re-establish this squadron as a fighter-bomber unit and re-equip it with aircraft delivered from the former USSR. Following extensive training in Russia and Ukraine, as well as in Iran, the 71st TFS became operational with the Su-24MK in 1994, and moved back to TFB.7 two years later.

Electronic Reconnaissance Squadron

The background to this unit was a series of top-secret joint operations between the IIAF, USAF, NSA and the CIA that began in the 1960s and culminated in the early 1970s. Most of these operations served the purpose of obtaining various forms of intelligence on the Soviet Union, but also on Iraq and several other Middle Eastern countries. In the early 1970s, the IIAF launched Project Ibex, worth over 500 million US Dollars at the time, and including not only the construction of an entire chain of SIGINT-collection ground stations, but also a number of correspondingly equipped aircraft. Within the framework of this project, the IIAF operated four C-130Hs and two Boeing 707-3J9Cs, supported by two Imperial Iranian Army Aviation (IIAA) Rockwell Commander 690As, modified by E-Systems' Greenville Division in the US.

Nicknamed Khofaash (Bat) in Iranian service, the resultant RC-130Hs (an unofficial designation) were equipped with a new navigational platform, as well as a number of detection and receiver antennae mounted around the fuselage and wings, plus consoles for 13 operators. These aircraft had entered operational service by 1975, and flew numerous missions – frequently staged from TFB.2 or TFB.3 – along the borders with the Soviet Union and Iraq, eavesdropping on local telecommunications. In 1978 two Khofaashs were reconfigured for transport duties, and during the Revolution of 1979, the American operators disabled much of the NSA-run Ibex ground equipment. Nevertheless, the two remaining RC-130s remained operational during the Iran-Iraq War, and proved exceptionally useful due to their capability to record most Iraqi military communications. Iraq launched a major effort to shoot one of these aircraft down, and repeatedly deployed its interceptors deep inside Iranian airspace. In due course, the Iraqi Air Force claimed to have downed no fewer than four Khofaash aircraft. Although at least one such claim did result in the shooting down of a regular Iranian transport, it is since known that the IRIAF still operates two RC-130s, as well as two Boeing 707-3J9Cs, one of which has meanwhile been reconverted to freighter standard.

The electronic reconnaissance fleet is still based at Mehrabad AB, and although its aircraft are regularly operated along Iranian borders (particularly by night), details of such operations remain a closely guarded secret.

12th Transport Aircraft Squadron

The original predecessor to this squadron came into being on 1 April 1949, as the 5th Transport Squadron, when the IIAF received its first C-47A/Bs. Except for flying ex-USAF C-47s during the 1950s and 1960s, this unit also received several Dakotas formerly flown by Iranian Airlines. In 1965, the 5th TAS received its first 4 C-130Bs, followed by 18 C-130Es and 23 C-130Hs. The availability of such a large number of C-130s resulted in a reorganisation of the IIAF's transport fleet. The 5th Squadron was re-designated as the 11th Transport Aircraft Squadron, and was joined by a second unit, the 12th Transport Aircraft Squadron, each nominally equipped with 12 C-130s.

Immediately after the Iraqi invasion, most of the C-130s from these two units were relocated to airfields in eastern Iran, from where they staged thousands of sorties in support of the ground forces, as well as IRIAF units. Indeed, the fleet was utilised so heavily that by the end of the war most of the remaining C-130s were in such a poor condition that the 11th TAS had to be disbanded.

Concentrated within the 12th TAS, the remaining aircraft have in recent years undergone complete overhaul at IACI's so-called 'C-130 Hangar' at Mehrabad. This facility remains the logistical and maintenance centre for the entire IRIAF C-130 fleet to this day.

Tanker and Transport Squadron

While going to great lengths to purchase over 200 F-4s and no less than 80 F-14s in the early 1970s, the IIAF also went to great efforts to obtain the ability to provide this large fleet of advanced fighters with tanker support. Launching Project Peace Station in 1974, the air force began purchasing nine Boeing 707-3J9C aircraft, this being the export variant of the Boeing KC-135A Stratotanker built for the USAF. Five additional 707s of the same variant were subsequently purchased, bringing the IIAF tanker squadron to full strength, some of these being equipped with wingtip-mounted pylons for the carriage of Beech 1800 in-flight refuelling pods, to enable refuelling of the Tomcat.

Meanwhile, in March 1975, the IIAF exploited the opportunity provided by the bankruptcy of TWA to acquire nine second-hand Boeing 747-131s (three of which were subsequently equipped as tanker aircraft by Boeing in Seattle), and three 747-124s in transport configuration. Although four of these aircraft were sold back to Boeing in 1978, the IIAF purchased five additional 747-2J9F freighters, equipped with upwards opening nose sections for rapid loading/offloading of large cargoes – a configuration that was to become standard fleet-wide. All the 707s and 747s entered service with a single unit based at TFB.1.

Following the Revolution, it was decided to donate all the expensive-to-operate 747s to the civilian national airline, Iran Air, or sell them back to the US. Since the primary purpose of these aircraft was hauling spare parts and carrying urgent weapons shipments in the case of a war with the USSR or Iraq, it was felt at the time that there was no longer any need for such a capability. However, the Iraqi invasion of 22 September 1980 proved how wrong such expectations were, and all the 707s and 747s were rushed back into service.

Throughout the war, the IRIAF tanker fleet flew on average five sorties a day, but often deployed up to eight 707s and three 747s to refuel F-4s on their way to Iraq, or F-4s/F-14s on combat air patrols within Iranian airspace. One 747-131 was usually deployed to transport arms and ammunition to airfields near the front line, and to evacuate badly wounded to the hospitals deeper inside Iran. Another 747-131 was equipped as an airborne command post, while several others completed their intended service, picking up arms shipments purchased by Iran from various countries around the world.

The IRIAF also launched its own airline, named Saha Air Lines, to transport civilian passengers on domestic routes, although priority was given to members of the military and their families. Practically every single IRIAF 707 and 747 served with Saha Air Lines at one point or another, but such intensive flying resulted in excessive wear and tear. By 2005, the IRIAF was left with only four 707-3J9C tankers, while most of the 747s were stored, awaiting spares and/or overhaul.

Given the poor shape of the fleet, the IRIAF command recently decided to launch a major effort to return as many aircraft to operational condition as possible.

By 2007 the Fajr-e Ashiyan Company, Iran Air and IACI at Mehrabad had overhauled one of the stored 747-131s and an ex-Iraqi Airways 747-

270C; another was overhauled in 2008, and additional examples followed thereafter. By spring 2009 the IRIAF was thus able to call upon seven 747-131s and one 747-270C, even though all the old aircraft experienced frequent technical problems and limited operability. Correspondingly, during summer 2009, Fajr-e Ashiyan was contracted to overhaul another stored 747-2J9F, which re-entered service in April 2010.

F27 Squadron

Although acquisition of C-130 transports by Iran began in the late 1960s, as of the early 1970s the backbone of the IIAF transport fleet still comprised the venerable C-47, purchased in sizeable numbers during the 1950s and 1960s. The type was cheap and easy to maintain and operate even under relatively primitive conditions. Nevertheless, in 1971 the air force decided to replace its remaining C-47s with a more modern type. Following a competition between two contenders, the Handley Page Herald and Fokker F27 Friendship, the latter type was chosen. Deliveries of 15 F27-400M Troopships (the military variant that was also built for the US Army) and five Fokker F27-600s (a cargo/passenger variant) took place between 11 February 1972 until 11 September 1974.

Initially based at Dowshan Tappeh AB, the emerging F27 Squadron also maintained a contingent deployed at Mehrabad, where they shared facilities with the VIP Squadron. In service with the IIAF, the F27 was primarily used to deploy paratroopers, and to transport spare parts, VIPs, personnel and families. An additional role was target towing. During the war with Iraq, the unit's F27s also saw widespread service transporting arms and supplies, as well as casualty evacuation. The flying was so intensive that by the late 1980s several airframes had to be grounded due to fatigue and corrosion problems.

In the early 1990s, the entire F27 fleet was relocated to Mehrabad in order to ease maintenance. Together with two Falcon 20Fs, one F27-400M was subsequently equipped with powerful cameras and saw extensive service for several years in support of the Armed Forces' Geographical Organisation.

While the diminishing F27 fleet continues to operate, the IRIAF is seeking to replace the worn-out type, perhaps with a military transport version of the Antonov/IAMI IrAn-140 Faraaz.

Falcon Star and VIP Transport Squadrons

The first time the IIAF allocated one of its transport aircraft specifically to the purpose of serving its commander-in-chief was in 1940. During the late 1940s and through the 1950s, the Shah of Iran frequently travelled in – and personally piloted – a privately owned Boeing B-17G Flying Fortress (EP-HIM), reconfigured for VIP transport during its previous demonstration service with TWA. Later on, IIAF commanders often used a C-47A (5-24), while another Dakota owned by Iran Air served members of the government before its replacement by a Vickers Viscount (839).

In the 1960s, Iran acquired a Lockheed L-1329 JetStar II to serve as VIP transport, subsequently reinforced through the addition of a single Boeing 727-81, operated by the 'Imperial Flight' at Mehrabad. In 1969 this aircraft was replaced by a single L-1329 JetStar VIII, based at Mehrabad and usually parked inside the so-called 'Imperial Hangar', together with a number of other aircraft and helicopters serving the government and the Imperial Court.

However, the Iranian government was clearly in need of a more versatile platform, and in order to avoid the use of the IIAF's valuable 707 tankers, in 1974 it acquired a former Iraqi Airways Boeing 707-370C and one Boeing 707-386C and converted them both for VIP transport. One additional JetStar II and three Dassault Falcon 20Fs followed two years later.

Although officially owned by the government and wearing civilian registrations, all these aircraft were maintained and flown by IIAF personnel. In the late 1970s they began receiving air force serial numbers and markings and the three Falcon 20Fs eventually entered service with the Falcon Star Squadron, which was mainly responsible for transporting high-ranking air force officers between various air bases, as well as radar and navigational system calibration.

Following the 1979 Revolution, the pair of 707s and the two JetStars of the former Imperial Flight were grounded until early 1980s, by which time the unit had been renamed as the 'Republic Flight'. The Falcon Star Squadron, however, had remained operational throughout, still primarily transporting IRIAF officers between various bases, but also saw some service for air ambulance work.

The IRIAF's VIP transport fleet was significantly reinforced in 1991 when two Iraqi Airways Falcon 50EXs, two Falcon 20Fs and one L-1329 JetStar II, as well as a heavily modified Iraqi Air Force Falcon 50EX (nicknamed Suzanna in Iraq) were evacuated to Iran. The fate of the latter, equipped with the Cyrano IVM targeting radar of the Dassault Mirage F.1EQ-5 fighter-bomber, and a full Mirage cockpit, additional fuel tanks inside the cabin, and the capability to carry up to two French-made AM.39 Exocet anti-ship missiles and a drop tank under the wings, remains unknown. Nevertheless, one JetStar and two Falcon 50s are known to have been allocated to the 'Republic Hangar' and are still used to transport members of the government and clergy, while the other aircraft entered service with the Falcon Star Squadron.

On 5 January 1995, the L-1329 JetStar II with the serial number 1003 was involved in a fatal crash, which killed the then C-in-C of the air force, and 12 other high-ranking IRIAF officers. The cause of the crash was determined to be structural failure. At the time of writing, only one Falcon 20F and two Falcon 50EXs remain in service with the Falcon Star Squadron, while the remaining JetStar is rarely flown. The VIP Transport Squadron housed in the 'Republic Hangar' operates two 707s, one Boeing 737-286C, one Airbus A321-231, and one Airbus A320-232.

11th Helicopter Transport Squadron

In 1963 the IIAF acquired its first helicopters, when 12 Sikorsky UH-19Ds arrived from the US. They entered service with the 1st Helicopter Squadron based at Mehrabad, even though at least one or two examples served as VIP transports and were permanently based at Dowshan Tappeh AB.

In 1968 the IIAF established a small VIP transport unit flying the UH-19D, which was subsequently reinforced through the acquisition of two Bell 206A Jet Rangers. Operated from Mehrabad, both Jet Rangers were later transferred to Imperial Iranian Police Aviation in the mid-1970s, and were replaced by two Agusta-Bell AB.212s.

In 1971 the IIAF received the first of 20 Boeing Vertol CH-47C Chinook heavy transport helicopters, built under license by Elicotteri-Meridionali in Italy. The Chinooks entered service with the reorganised 11th Helicopter Transport Squadron, allowing retirement of the entire UH-19D fleet. Before long, 15 of the IIAF Chinooks were handed over to the IIAA, and thus only five (according to some reports, only two) examples remained in air force service during the 1970s. The survivors were mainly used by the IIAF for crash recovery, SAR and transport of bulky payloads. The squadron was reinforced in 1981, however, when it received two newly built examples from Italy, these helicopters including anti-FOD screens on the engine intakes and redesigned rotor blades.

Following the Islamic Revolution of 1979 and during the war with Iraq, the CH-47Cs of the 11th Helicopter Transport Squadron saw extensive service at various battlefields in support of Iranian ground forces. The helicopters were also used in support of the work of the IRIAF's Self-Sufficiency Jihad Directorate (SSJD), an industrial-research unit responsible for reverse engineering and manufacturing spare parts and weapons for the air force. In this role, the IRIAF's Chinooks mainly transported damaged aircraft and helicopters between various air bases, or even large pieces of airframe wreckage. These items were usually collected at Mehrabad and stored for subsequent repairs or for cannibalisation as spare parts.

Only four IRIAF Chinooks were operational by 2000, but thereafter one helicopter after another had to be withdrawn from service due to their increasingly poor condition. By 2007 only one Chinook remained in service, prompting the IRIAF to launch a project to return some of the stored airframes to service. However, the project has progressed slowly and only one Chinook has been completely rebuilt and returned to operational condition, in 2008.

Interestingly, for most of the 1980s Iranian VIPs travelled in IRIAA AB.214s or IRIAF AB.214Cs from TFB.1's SAR Squadron. However, in 1995 the Islamic government acquired three Bell 412s, four Bell 212s and one Bell 206L-4 Long Ranger from Bell Textron of Canada, these being transported to Iran in Russian Antonov An-124s. Except for the single Long Ranger, all of these helicopters were assigned to the 'Republic Hangar' at Mehrabad. Although painted in colours very similar to those of Bell 214Cs operated by the IRIAF, and maintained by air force personnel, these helicopters are almost exclusively for VIP transport use. As such, they are modified with the latest navigational aids and can often be seen carrying the leader or the president of the Islamic Republic during visits to various parts of the country, or even for travelling within the capital city.

Mehrabad SAR Squadron

In the 1960s the IIAF obtained at least 32 Kaman HH-43F Husky helicopters for base SAR and firefighting duties. The aircraft were received through MAP. Initially based at Mehrabad AB, they were subsequently distributed within two SAR units, the second of which was based at Dezful. However, as additional air bases were constructed during the 1970s, more SAR squadrons – or rather flights – were established, with smaller number of airframes per unit. Correspondingly, in 1968 the IIAF acquired 12 Bell UH-1D Iroquois helicopters. By 1973 the largest SAR units of the IIAF were stationed at Mehrabad and Shiraz, where all associated maintenance facilities were also established. The Huskies' days in Iran soon came to an end, as they were – arguably prematurely – replaced by 39 Bell Textron Model 214Cs, which entered service in 1976 and 1977. The new helicopters not only served with units based at TFB.1 and TFB.7, but also at TFB.2 and TFB.4.

Bell 214Cs saw extensive service during the war with Iraq, rescuing dozens of downed Iranian airmen – several of them from behind enemy lines. Attrition was heavy as a result, with more than half of the Bell 214C and AB.205/UH-1D fleet being lost in combat or in the course of various accidents. This eventually prompted the IRIAF to refurbish and return to service 10 stored HH-43Fs. Most of the UH-1Ds had either been lost or were worn out and retired by the early 1990s, followed by the HH-43Fs, which were withdrawn from service between 1990 and 1992. The IRIAF subsequently decided to pool all its remaining Bell 214Cs – less than a dozen airframes in total – within just two units, one based at Mehrabad and the other at Shiraz.

IRIAF 2010

TFB.1 Mehrabad

IRIAF 2010

MiG-29 3-6132 is towed away following engine tests at the 11th TFS ramp on the northeast side of TFB.1. This is one of four ex-Iraqi MiG-29s flown to Iran on 26 January 1991. It was completely overhauled before entering IRIAF service.
(Babak Taghvaee)

MiG-29s 3-6132 and 3-6305 make a low pass over Runway 29L at Mehrabad AB. Both aircraft sport freshly applied air defence camouflage, received during periodic maintenance.
(Babak Taghvaee) ◄

MiG-29UB 3-6305 on finals at Mehrabad following a training sortie. This aircraft underwent periodic maintenance in summer 2007, during which it received new navigational aids and other avionics.
(Babak Taghvaee)

TFB.1 Mehrabad

3-6117 is another MiG-29 operated by the 11th TFS. It is seen on finals at Mehrabad while returning from a visual weather-check sortie. Notable is the armament of four R-73 (AA-11 Archer) air-to-air missiles.
(Babak Taghvaee)

MiG-29UB 3-6306 on finals at Mehrabad AB. During the landing, the left engine is on idle while the right engine is set at slightly more than 60 per cent power.
(Babak Taghvaee)

IRIAF 2010

TFB.1 Mehrabad

IRIAF 2010

TFB.1 still frequently hosts much activity, although not on the scale of the 1970s. MiG-29 3-6117 is seen landing on Runway 29L, while 3-6132 and MiG-29UB 3-6305 are towed away after training flights, and a C-130H of the 12th TAS prepares for take-off.
(Babak Taghvaee)

MiG-29 3-6114 lands on Mehrabad AB's Runway 29L. The aircraft was armed with two R-27R (AA-10 Alamo) and two R-73 (AA-11 Archer) air-to-air missiles since it was flying an escort sortie for the aircraft carrying the Supreme Leader of the Revolution, Ali Khamenei, during a visit to Noshahr.
(Babak Taghvaee) ◄

TFB.1 Mehrabad

3-6114 is another single-seat MiG-29 in service with the 11th TFS. On this occasion it was shown together with dummy R-27 (left) and R-73 (right) missiles.
(Liam F. Devlin)

In recent years, MiG-29UB 3-6306 has been one of most active two-seaters in the 11th TFS. As this book went to press, the aircraft was undergoing periodical checks and an upgrade.
(Liam F. Devlin)

31

C-130E 5-8503 on Runway 29L prior to take-off. Back in the 1970s, while still wearing the serial number 5-107, this aircraft was operated by the 71st TAS from TFB.7. At the time of writing it was undergoing overhaul at Mehrabad.
(Babak Taghvaee)

5-8503 rolls down Runway 15 at Mehrabad AB.
(Babak Taghvaee)

TFB.1 Mehrabad

IRIAF 2010

C-130H 5-8538 has been one of most active Hercules of the 12th TAS in recent years. The IRIAF Hercules fleet was long absent from TFB.1 during the war with Iraq, most aircraft being evacuated to airfields in the east of the country.
(Babak Taghvaee)

5-8538 about to touch down at Mehrabad AB, against a backdrop of the Alborz Mountains and an IRGC-operated Il-76.
(Babak Taghvaee) ◀

TFB.1 Mehrabad

After being stored for some years, following its overhaul at Mehrabad, C-130H 5-8551 is now one of the most active aircraft of this type. Delivered to Iran in May 1975, it is equipped with more advanced navigational systems than most other C-130s in IRIAF service.
(Babak Taghvaee)

IRIAF 2010

5-8503 on take-off from TFB.1, against the backdrop of the ramp shared by the 12th TAS and the F27 Squadron. (Ali Heydari)

TFB.1 Mehrabad

One of three CH-47Cs currently operational with the IRIAF's 11th HTS. For years, 5-9304 was the only Chinook active with this unit, as other examples were stored due to a lack of finances and spare parts.
(Liam F. Devlin)

CH-47C 5-9303 was stored for some years before being overhauled and returned to service in 2008.
(Liam F. Devlin)

After almost a year of complex overhauls at the helicopter works in Penha, 5-9305 rejoined the operational fleet with the 11th HTS in March 2009.
(Babak Taghvaee)

TFB.1 Mehrabad

In the 1970s the Iranian Air Force upgraded two of its Boeing 707s as SIGINT-gathering aircraft under Project Ibex, undertaken jointly with SAVAK, the NSA and the CIA. One of these remains in service today.
(Ali Heydari)

A detail study of the SIGINT-collecting equipment installed in the forward fuselage of Boeing 707 5-8316. The other Boeing 707 equipped with similar systems had to be withdrawn from service because of fatigue endured in the course of extensive operations during the war with Iraq.
(Ali Heydari)

IRIAF 2010

40

TFB.1 Mehrabad

5-8554

IRIAF 2010

From a fleet of no less than 14 Boeing 707 transport and tanker aircraft acquired in the 1970s, the IRIAF nowadays operates only two aircraft of this type, including 5-8304, a Boeing 707-3J9C (an export variant of the KC-135A tanker), and one example equipped for SIGINT duties.
(Ali Heydari)

Although looking like any other C-130 in IRIAF service, 5-8554 is one of two examples locally nicknamed Khofaash (Bat). These aircraft were equipped as SIGINT collectors under Project Ibex in the mid-1970s.
(Ali Heydari) ◄

TFB.1 Mehrabad

Of the last three Boeing 707-3J9C tankers in IRIAF service, two examples (including 5-8306 shown here) were converted to passenger aircraft in 2007 and since then have been operated by Saha Air Lines.
(Liam F. Devlin)

The last Boeing 707-3J9C on finals at Mehrabad AB. The aircraft is mainly flown for transport duties, but it can be relatively quickly converted back to tanker configuration. Notable are the Beech 1800 refuelling pods, carried under the wingtips, used to provide fuel to F-14s and Su-24s.
(Ali Heydari) ▶

43

IRIAF 2010

TFB.1 Mehrabad

Boeing 747-2J9F 5-8115 is a transport variant and was delivered to Iran in 1977. Initially serving with Saha, it was returned to IRIAF service in 1987, and was used to fly SS-1 Scud-C surface-to-surface missiles from North Korea during the same year.
(Ali Heydari)

TFB.1 Mehrabad

Boeing 747-131 tanker 5-8103 takes off from Mehrabad against the backdrop of the ramp occupied by the 1st Transport Base. Only a few years ago, this was the only airworthy 747 tanker in IRIAF service. Two more have since been overhauled and returned to service, and 5-8103 has been undergoing overhaul at the Fajr Ashian company since 2009.
(Ali Heydari)

Boeing 747-131 tanker 5-8107 lands following a post-overhaul test flight. The aircraft required very extensive works to be returned to service, these being completed between mid-2007 and March 2009.
(Ali Heydari) ▶

IRIAF 2010

TFB.1 Mehrabad

The Iranian Air Force once operated a sizeable fleet of Fokker F27s, including this example equipped as a passenger transport, and stored at TFB.1 for some years. (Liam F. Devlin)

One of two F27-400Ms – 5-8804 (seen here) and 5-8817 – equipped with long focal length cameras for mapping purposes. (Ali Heydari)

TFB.1 Mehrabad

Formerly a part of the Imperial Flight of the IIAF, and now serving with the Republic Flight, this Lockheed L-1329 JetStar II is the only example remaining in service with the VIP Transport Squadron. Since the crash of an ex-Iraqi example in 1995, however, it has been flown only very rarely.
(Liam F. Devlin)

This Dassault Falcon 20F, formerly YI-AHH, previously served with Iraqi Airways, before it took refugee in Iran on 26 January 1991. It was assigned the IRIAF serial number 5-9014. Equipped with a long focal length camera, it currently serves with the Iran National Cartographic Centre for topography and cartography purposes.
(Liam F. Devlin)

51

IRIAF 2010

The two Boeing 707s of the IRIAF's VIP Transport Squadron (serial number 1002 is seen here) regularly fly various high-ranking politicians and dignitaries around the country and also during visits abroad.
(Babak Taghvaee)

TFB.1 Mehrabad

The VIP Squadron operates two Boeing 707s equipped as VIP passenger aircraft, one of which (serial number 1001) is seen on finals at Mehrabad AB. (Babak Taghvaee)

This Falcon 50 is one of two ex-Iraqi Air Force/Iraqi Airways aircraft of this type flown to Iran from Iraq in January 1991. It remains in service with the Falcon Squadron as a light VIP transport, and is foremost used by leading military officers of the Islamic Republic. (Babak Taghvaee)

Bell 214A 4-4939 has been in service with the Mehrabad SAR Squadron since its delivery in 1977. The same unit also operates several examples of the more powerful Bell 214C.
(Liam F. Devlin)

Tactical Fighter Base 2 Tabriz

The city of Tabriz in northwest Iran has had an airstrip since 1948. In 1954 the facility received its first navigational aids, after which it was officially designated as Tabriz Airport. Two years later, the first administrative buildings and a tower were erected, and Iran Air established a regular service between Tehran and Tabriz.

Development of a military section of the airport began only in 1960, when the remaining F-84Gs and P-47Ds of the former 1st and 3rd FS were deployed there. Later, the military side of Tabriz airport was designated as a tactical fighter base, however, Tabriz Airport remained a predominantly civilian installation, and changed very little even after the F-84Gs and P-47Ds had been successively replaced by F-86Fs between 1966 and 1968.

Considering Tabriz's proximity to the Soviet borders, in 1970 the IIAF decided to expand the local facilities and establish a fully developed air base. Most of the relevant work – including the lengthening of the main runway and construction of a second runway, as well as construction of administrative, maintenance and storage buildings – was complete by 1971. Tabriz was then officially declared as the 5th Tactical Fighter Base (TFB.5), and become home to two F-5A squadrons, the 501st and 502nd TFS. These two units were further reinforced through the addition of a COIN squadron equipped with 12 Cessna O-2A light attack and forward air control aircraft.

In the course of the IIAF's reorganisation in 1974, Tabriz air base was re-designated as TFB.2. Correspondingly, the 501st and 502nd TFS were re-designated as the 21st and 22nd TFS. In the following years, both squadrons began replacing their F-5As with the newly delivered Northrop F-5E/F Tiger II fighter-bombers, the numbers of which eventually grew to a level where a third unit, the 23rd TFS, could be established. Despite such growth, and the fact that Tabriz was repeatedly used for the forward deployment of reconnaissance aircraft from Mehrabad, TFB.2 remained one of the smallest Iranian air bases until the mid-1970s. It was only then that construction of hardened aircraft shelters for 80 fighters and a separate military ramp suitable for handling the heaviest IIAF transport aircraft was completed. Subsequently, TFB.2 was reinforced through the addition of Raytheon MIM-23 HAWK and BAC Rapier SAM batteries, as well as Oerlikon Contraves radar-assisted anti-aircraft gun systems. Meanwhile, a SAR Squadron equipped with six helicopters took over the role of base search and rescue.

By 1979, in the aftermath of the Revolution that briefly saw the base renamed as Jānbāz, the three locally based F-5 squadrons each had at least 20 Tigers. All three units flew intensive combat sorties against Iraq from the start of the war in September 1980. Most of these missions were directed at Iraqi air bases as well as strategic oil facilities.

Despite considerable successes – including the downing of an Iraqi Mikoyan i Gurevich MiG-25 interceptor with 20mm cannon on 3 July 1986 – losses were heavy, with more than 50 per cent of the 'Tabrizi' F-5E/Fs being written off by 1988. The situation eventually resulted in the decision to re-organise the 21st and 22nd TFS as a single unit in 1990. One year later, the 23rd TFS was re-equipped with MiG-29s after its pilots completed their training on the new type at Mehrabad.

More recently, the IRIAF units based at TFB.2 have been reinforced through the addition of a unit equipped with several overhauled and upgraded F-5Es, named Saegheh. Within the IRIAF, the operating unit for these aircraft is simply known as the Saegheh Squadron.

21st Tactical Fighter Squadron

The current 21st TFS draws its legacy from two former F-5E/F units, the 21st and 22nd TFS, and formerly operated just over 20 aircraft of this type, before a decision was made to reassign several of them to TFB.14 (see the relevant section for details). Although old and fatigued, the F-5E/Fs of the 21st TFS are in considerably better condition than aircraft of this type in service with other units. It is for this reason that several TFB.2 aircraft have been used for a number of development projects since the mid-1990s.

These have included installation of in-flight refuelling probes on a small number of F-5Es and F-5Fs, while others have tested the Russian-made R-60MK (AA-8 Aphid) and the Chinese-made PL-7 air-to-air missiles. To this day, the 21st TFS remains the largest Iranian F-5 unit.

23rd Tactical Fighter Squadron

Negotiations between Iran and the then Soviet Union for the acquisition of a number of MiG-29 fighter jets began in early 1989, and the first from a total of 18 aircraft arrived at TFB.1 in June the following year, initially entering service with the 11th TFS. Although Iran lacked the finances to acquire a sufficient number of MiG-29s to form another unit, four additional MiG-29s were evacuated to Iran from Iraq in 1991, and it was decided to split the available aircraft between TFB.1 and TFB.2. In the process, the 23rd TFS was reorganised as the second unit flying the type.

Interestingly, although all MiG-29s have undergone overhauls in recent years, those operated from Tabriz retained their original camouflage colours and pattern, as applied for their delivery in 1990.

Saegheh Squadron

Project Saegheh was launched by the Iranian defence ministry in the mid-1990s, as an offshoot of Project Azarakhsh, and these ultimately aimed towards a complete overhaul and considerable upgrade of the remaining F-5E/F fleet. Initially, the intention was to undertake overhauls and manufacture spares. At some point in time, this idea evolved to encompass domestic 'series production' of a much modified 'new' aircraft based on existing fuselages. Local production would be entrusted to Iranian Aircraft Manufacturing Industries (IAMI, or Hessa in Persian) at Shahin-Shahr near Esfahan. Following a prolonged research and development phase, the initial Saegheh prototype flew for the first time from Shahin-Shahr airport in 2002, with the second and third prototypes following in summer 2007. While the first Saegheh prototype included considerably redesigned intakes and nose radome, in addition to twin canted fins, all subsequent aircraft retained the basic F-5E fuselage with the exception of the twin fins, which were now attached to the rear fuselage using a simpler and lighter composite fairing.

By 2009 Hessa had completed a total of five Saeghehs, enabling the establishment of a small squadron. The unit first moved from Shahin-Shahr to Mehrabad, and then to TFB.2 in September of the same year. In the future, the Saegheh Squadron is likely to be further augmented through the addition of more aircraft, since this project is expected to continue for some time.

TFB.2 Tabriz

F-5s of the 21st TFS (foreground) frequently conduct joint exercises with MiG-29s of the 23rd TFS (background). This photograph was taken during an IRIAF gunnery competition (usually named Fedayeen-e-Asseman-e-Velayat, or Immolates of Velayat's Sky).
(IRIAF)

IRIAF 2010

Veteran of many daring combat missions flown during the war with Iraq, and pending an overhaul at IACI, F-5E 3-7507 soldiers on with the 21st TFS after more than 30 years.
(Liam F. Devlin)

F-5E 3-7335 is the former 3-7077. It was photographed during final checks before take-off from Mehrabad AB for participation in a military parade over the Iranian capital.
(Babak Taghvaee)

TFB.2 Tabriz

F-5s require a minimum of maintenance and although they are put through periodic overhaul, most of the aircraft in IRIAF service still wear the same camouflage applied before their delivery, in the mid-1970s.
(Babak Taghvaee)

F-5F 3-7167 is one of only a handful of two-seat Tiger IIs still assigned to the 21st TFS. The aircraft was photographed over Tehran during the Holy Defence Week Parade on 22 September 2009.
(Babak Taghvaee)

59

Fully armed MiG-29 3-6112 returns from a combat air patrol along the borders with Iraq and Turkey. The armament comprises a pair of R-27R and R-73 air-to-air missiles. (IRIAF)

TFB.2 Tabriz

MiG-29 3-6103 formerly served with the 11th TFS at Mehrabad AB, but was recently relocated to the 23rd TFS.
(Babak Taghvaee)

MiG-29UB 3-6301 has served with the 23rd TFS since the type entered IRIAF service in early 1991.
(Babak Taghvaee)

61

The Saeqeh fighter emerged as a result of various projects for the upgrade of surviving IRIAF F-5E/F fighters. This photograph shows the original first prototype (S110-001), which includes a deeper front fuselage and square intakes.
(Babak Taghvaee)

Four Saeqehs line up during final checks before take-off from Mehrabad AB, in September 2009, prior to their participation in the military parade over the Iranian capital.
(Babak Taghvaee)

TFB.2 Tabriz

Saeqeh 3-7367 was the second prototype, and is representative of the standard to which all subsequent examples have been configured.
(Babak Taghvaee)

3-7368 was the fourth Saeqeh built, and it joined the fleet in early 2009. The type represents a rebuild of older, damaged or worn-out F-5E fuselages to a new standard. The Saeqeh is equipped with twin fins but lacks wingtip launch rails for Sidewinder air-to-air missiles.
(Babak Taghvaee)

IRIAF 2010

TFB.2 Tabriz

IRIAF 2010

Illustrating all F-5 variants currently in IRIAF service, this photograph was taken in September 2009 at Mehrabad AB. It shows (from left to right), a Saeqeh fighter, an F-5F from TFB.2 and another from TFB.4, an F-5B Simourgh (painted white overall), and one of only two examples of the F-5F Azarakhsh that have entered service to date (painted green overall).
(Babak Taghvaee) ◄

Tactical Fighter Base 3 Nojeh

The construction of the future Shahrokhi 3rd Tactical Fighter Base (TFB.3, named after Col Nasrollah Shahrokhi, who was killed in a jet crash in 1950) began in 1963. At this time the IIAF made the decision to establish a major military airfield at a strategic location opposite the Iraqi border in west-central Iran. The location selected was a site outside the village of Kaboudar-Ahang, near the city of Hamedan. From the start, TFB.3 was designed as a 'strategic' air base and was extensively equipped. Nevertheless, the first military aircraft based there were the F-86Fs of the former 101st TFS. These arrived at TFB.3 in January 1965, after they had been replaced at Mehrabad by newly delivered F-5As.

Following the delivery of additional F-5A/Bs, in 1966 and 1967 three units were established at TFB.3, these comprising the 301st, 302nd and 303rd TFS, each operating a total of 16 aircraft. The facilities constructed at TFB.3 were so vast that at least two F-5s could be parked inside every hardened aircraft shelter constructed on the northern side of the base. Subsequently, additional hardened shelters – capable of accommodating up to four F-5s – were constructed on the southeast side of the base, and the facility received protection in the form of Shorts Tigercat SAMs and Oerlikon anti-aircraft guns.

During the mid-1970s, F-4Es and MIM-23B I-HAWK SAMs replaced F-5A/Bs and Tigercats, respectively, while in 1974 the three locally based fighter squadrons were re-designated as the 31st, 32nd and 33rd TFS. By 1978, the composition of the units based at Shahrokhi remained the same, each squadron having some 17 F-4Es at its disposal.

The base was the scene of political unrest during and immediately after the 1979 Revolution, and most of its aircraft were stored. In the summer of the same year, however, personnel from Shahrokhi were among the first to reactivate, to help quell a Kurdish uprising in northwest Iran. Due to a lack of proficiency flying and a breakdown of standard maintenance procedures caused by the maintainers' frequent strike actions, the first F-4E to take off on such a sortie, flown by Capt Mohamad Nojeh, crashed, killing its crew. As a result, Shahrokhi air base was renamed Nojeh.

During summer 1980 several purged and active TFB.3 officers, together with elements of the Iranian special forces, the 65th Paratroop Brigade in Shiraz, the Ahwaz 92nd Armoured Division and other units, were involved in the plotting of a major coup against the new government in Tehran. This coup attempt, commonly known as the 'Nojeh Plan', had far-reaching consequences. When it was uncovered, all the officers involved were arrested and executed or imprisoned, and the entire IRIAF promptly came under even greater scrutiny from the authorities. This resulted in widespread purges and the near demobilisation of the entire service.

Nevertheless, from the afternoon of 22 September 1980, Nojeh became the front-line air base of the war with Iraq. Although attacked at least a dozen times by Iraqi fighter-bombers, it was the first base to launch retaliatory raids against Iraq, on the same afternoon. Furthermore, on the morning of 23 September, TFB.3 launched no less than 48 F-4Es to attack Iraqi military installations as part of the famous 140-aircraft raid, Operation Kaman-99. Although repeated Iraqi air attacks caused the losses of several Phantoms in the following weeks, the air base remained the main hub of the IRIAF's long-range combat operations. TFB.3 launched a large number of highly successful sorties against targets in the Baghdad area, but also struck targets as deep as Kirkuk in northern Iraq (in autumn 1980), and even H-3 air base, in the farthest reaches of western Iraq (April 1981).

In late January and through February 1991, TFB.3 was the main destination for Iraqi Air Force aircraft escaping the wrath of Operation Desert Storm. More than 90 Iraqi fighters and fighter-bombers took refuge at the base, in addition to more than 20 transport and commercial aircraft. Many of them – including four Sukhoi Su-20s, more than 16 Su-22M-2K/M-3K/M-4K and Su-22UMs, seven Mirage F.1s, and two damaged Su-24MKs – are still parked in and around hardened aircraft shelters on the northern side of the base.

Following the arrival of the first MiG-29s in Iran in June 1990, the remaining F-4Es of the 11th TFS, as well as all the remaining RF-4s of the 11th TRS, were reassigned to units at Nojeh. However, the total number of operational Phantoms had decreased to such a degree that the 33rd TFS had to be disbanded. As a result, currently only the 31st and 32nd TFS remain operational with F-4Es.

31st and 32nd Tactical Fighter Squadrons

Originally established as the 301st and 302nd TFS, these two units used to fly 16 F-5A/Bs delivered in 1966 and 1967. By 1973, together with their sister unit, the 303rd TFS, they operated no less than 43 F-5As and 16 F-5Bs, before a decision was made to re-equip the squadrons with F-4Es. Immediately afterwards, 41 F-5As and 9 F-5Bs from the Shahrokhi inventory – these were technically still US government property – were redelivered to South Vietnam. Later, six F-5As (including four aircraft from other IIAF bases) and one F-5B were redelivered to Ethiopia. Subsequently, each Shahrokhi squadron received 16 F-4Es, as well as four reserve airframes.

Beginning in late March 1971, the 31st TFS also began operating the RF-4 reconnaissance variant of the Phantom II. Among these were at least two RF-4Cs delivered directly from USAF stocks and flown by US crews on several secret reconnaissance sorties over Iraq in October 1973. One of these aircraft was shot down over the USSR in November of the same year, while flown by a mixed Iranian-American crew.

Subsequently reinforced through the acquisition of additional RF-4Es, the 31st TFS represented the most important reconnaissance asset of the IRIAF during the early stages of the war with Iraq. However, most of the 31st TFS reconnaissance aircraft were lost in the course of the conflict, and had to be replaced by RF-4s from the 11th TRS, based at Mehrabad.

Operating from TFB.3, F-4 Phantoms flew hundreds of critically important 'special missions' (SM) over Iraq. Following early counter-air attacks on airfields in the Baghdad area, they also bombed the construction site of the nuclear reactors in Tuwaitha, in the southern suburbs of the Iraqi capital, on 30 September 1980. They then expanded their list of targets to include oil facilities in northern as well as in southern Iraq. In October 1980, Phantom pilots of the 31st, 32nd and 33rd TFS flew a series of daring mass raids against targets in the Baghdad area. These strikes left lasting impressions upon the local population and soon became known as the 'Baghdad Express' among foreign correspondents witnessing their low-level manoeuvrings over Baghdad. As well as participating in the massive battle for Khuzestan, which raged through the rest of the year, battle-hardened F-4E pilots from TFB.3 also conducted the famous 'H-3 Blitz' on 1 April 1981. In the course of this mission a formation of Phantoms supported by tanker aircraft crossed the expanses of northern and northwest Iraq to reach the H-3 complex of three air bases in western Iraq, near the Jordanian border. After hitting their targets, the Phantoms returned unmolested.

In the subsequent years Nojeh's F-4E squadrons produced some of the most famous Iranian air warfare tacticians. These pilots stood out on account of their courage in combat, and the skills they displayed in flying their big, powerful and heavy fighter-bombers at very low level along uncharted routes deep into Iraq. Perhaps the most famous was Lt Col Abbas Dowran, who personally flew dozens of SMs. After outsmarting Iraqi air defences dozens of times, Dowran was finally shot down and killed over central Baghdad in late June 1982. Today, a number of murals depicting Dowran and other heroes of TFB.3 decorate walls around the city of Hamedan, and also Tehran.

During the war, almost half of all the F-4s stationed at TFB.3 were lost, together with most of the base's RF-4s. Correspondingly, in autumn 1980 the majority of the Phantoms operated by the 91st and 92nd TFS at Bandar Abbas TFMB.9 were redeployed to TFB.3. In return, when most of the pilots and maintainers of the two TFMB.9 squadrons were killed in a C-130E crash in winter 1988, a new 91st TFS was formed from units and aircraft previously assigned to Nojeh's 31st and 32nd TFS.

Today, the 31st and 32nd TFS remain the largest F-4 squadrons within the IRIAF, operating not only F-4Es but also all the remaining RF-4s.

TFB.3 Nojeh

The mighty F-4E Phantom II remains the backbone of the IRIAF fighter fleet.
(IRIAF)

3-6652 was one of four F-4Es from TFB.3 that participated in an IRIAF gunnery competition at Tabriz in 2009. The aircraft is a veteran of more than 200 combat sorties over Iraq (including at least 30 over Baghdad) and a confirmed multiple 'MiG-killer'.
(Babak Taghvaee)

Another F-4E still serving at TFB.3 is 3-6684, one of the last Phantoms delivered to Iran. This aircraft is known to have flown over 400 combat sorties against Iraq and to have scored at least one confirmed MiG-21 kill, in 1981. Note that it is equipped with the TISEO internal TV camera set.
(Babak Taghvaee)

TFB.3 Nojeh

All IRIAF fighter-bomber units undertake regular bombing exercises, often far away from their bases. This F-4E is seen taking off from TFB.3 and carries a SUU-10/A practice bomb dispenser under its starboard underwing pylon.
(Babak Taghvaee)

IRIAF 2010

RF-4C 2-6504 was the fourth reconnaissance Phantom officially delivered to Iran. It originally served with the 11th TRS at Mehrabad AB, until that unit was disbanded and all surviving RF-4s assigned to TFB.3.
(Liam F. Devlin)

One of the RF-4s still operational is 2-6504, now wearing this attractive camouflage pattern otherwise applied to Iranian F-14s.
(Babak Taghvaee)

Tactical Fighter Base 4 Vahdati

Dezful was only the second military airfield ever built in Iran. The facility was constructed as a small service airfield outside the town of Dezful in 1947 when Iran was in the process of receiving 60 P-47Ds. It then became the home base of one squadron (established in 1950) flying the Thunderbolt, as well as the 2nd Fighter Squadron, then equipped with the Hurricane Mk IIC. By 1961, Dezful airfield was officially designated as Vahdati 2nd Tactical Fighter Base (TFB.2), in honour of the Vahdati brothers, who were killed in an air accident. The local units were reorganised as the 201st and 202nd TFS and re-equipped with F-84Gs. While this process was under way, the final IIAF P-47D squadron – the then 4th TFS – moved to the airfield from Ghaleh-Morghi, and was given the task of air base defence.

In the mid-1960s, when Mehrabad-based units began re-equipping with F-86F Sabres, the 4th TFS was reorganised to form two new units, the 203rd TFS and 204th TFS, both of which flew F-84Gs. Similarly, when the first F-5A/Bs arrived at Mehrabad, in January 1965, the 201st and 202nd TFS re-equipped with Sabres. By 1971, a total of 42 F-86Fs were available, when the decision was taken to re-equip all four units with Freedom Fighters. In the process of this development, the 201st and 202nd TFS received 16 F-5As each, while the 203rd and 204th TFS merged to form the 203rd Tactical Training Squadron, which became an operational conversion unit equipped with 16 F-5Bs. The 203rd TTS – nicknamed 'Tigers' – was one of the most important IIAF units of the time, conducting fast-jet training for large numbers of novice pilots. Indeed, most of the future officers and commanders of the Iranian Air Force passed though this unit at some stage of their career. Additionally, in 1965 a SAR squadron was established at Vahdati, initially equipped with eight HH-43F helicopters.

Another reorganisation and re-equipment period followed in 1973 and 1974. Vahdati AB was officially re-designated as the 4th Tactical Fighter Base (TFB.4), while the 201st, 202nd and 203rd TFS became the 41st and 42nd TFS and the 43rd TTS, respectively. These units were subsequently re-equipped with 70 F-5E/Fs between them.

The 43rd TTS remained an important schoolhouse unit, as the pace of training operations increased and local instructors became involved in the establishment of a number of new F-5 units, with the IIAF awaiting the arrival of the General Dynamics F-16A/B Fighting Falcon, deliveries of which were slated to begin in 1979. Meanwhile, the locally based SAR squadron was re-equipped with Bell 214Cs.

Vahdati was also home to the IIAF's Golden Crown aerial demonstration team, equipped initially with F-84s, then F-86s, F-5As and finally F-5Es. These aircraft were flown by the best IIAF pilots and performed on countless occasions. Following the Revolution, however, the Golden Crown team was disbanded and its aircraft were returned to normal squadron duties.

TFB.4 remained largely untouched by the Revolution, even though its operational tempo was adversely affected. Therefore, when Iraq invaded Iran, the 41st and 42nd TFS were fully operational with 20 F-5E/Fs each, while the 43rd TTS operated an even larger number of F-5Bs and F-5Fs. These were soon reinforced by several RF-5As from the 11th TRS to fulfil reconnaissance duties.

From the first day of the war all three units found themselves in the midst of the struggle for Khuzestan. On 23 September 1980 the units launched 40 F-5E/Fs to participate in the famous 140-aircraft raid on Iraq. Losses were exceptionally heavy, and in addition, Vahdati came not only under attack from Iraqi surface-to-surface missiles and artillery, but also found itself on the receiving end of a major Iraqi Army offensive, in October 1980. The latter forced the IRIAF to partially evacuate the base. Operations continued, nevertheless, and by late 1980 Vahdati was not only back to its full strength through the addition of F-5E/Fs originally planned to enter service at TFB.5 and TFB.10, but was also reinforced through the forward deployment of Phantoms from TFB.6 and TFB.7. Vahdati remained operational throughout the entire war, even in the face of two more major Iraqi Air Force offensives directed against it, undertaken in autumn 1986 and autumn 1987.

Losses were correspondingly heavy; up to 51 of TFB.4's F-5Es and F-5Fs were shot down, and 20 others were badly damaged by 1988. Indeed, even when the local squadrons took over all the Tigers from the 51st, 52nd and 53rd TFS, there were not enough aircraft left to populate the three units. As a result, the 41st and 42nd TFS merged in 1990.

41st Tactical Fighter Squadron

The current 41st TFS came into being in 1990 through the merger of two veteran Iranian Air Force units, the 41st and 42nd TFS. Originally established in 1948, though under a previous designation, the 41st flew P-47Ds, F-84Gs, F-86Fs and then F-5A/Bs before re-equipping with F-5E/Fs in 1974.

This squadron suffered particularly heavy losses during the first days of the war with Iraq, and had to be temporarily reinforced by six F-5Es from TFB.2 in October and November 1980.

Today the 41st TFS still operates F-5E/Fs, even though most are in poor condition, and the unit is meanwhile one of the few within the IRIAF to sport large, colourful artworks on its aircraft's fins.

43rd Tactical Fighter Squadron

Previously operating 25 F-84Gs and later F-86Fs while still designated as the 203rd TFS, the future 43rd TFS came into being through a merger of the then 203rd TFS and the 204th TFS, when they re-equipped with F-5Bs, in 1971. During the late 1970s more than half of 43rd TTS F-5Bs and F-5Fs were temporarily assigned to TFB.10 in Chabahar, where they were used to train additional pilots.

After being reinforced through the addition of aircraft and pilots from the 21st, 22nd, 51st, 52nd and 53rd TFS, the squadron played a very active role during the early weeks of the war with Iraq. In 1981, the unit was again reorganised as a training outfit, and played an important role in re-training a number of transport pilots for fast-jet operations in order to replace wartime attrition. The unit lost its operational conversion role with the establishment of the IRIAF Academy at TFB.8 in 1985-86, and handed over all its remaining F-5Bs to the units based there.

Nevertheless, the 43rd TFS was subsequently assigned the role of the IRIAF Combat Commander School, and continues to operate F-5Es and F-5Fs alongside the 41st TFS.

TFB.4 Vahdati

Compared to F-5Es from TFB.2, the Tiger IIs from Vahdati AB can foremost be recognised by the darker green shade applied as part of their camouflage (in addition to the usual 'TFB/TAB number', applied in black, inside a small black circle, on either side of the fin).
(Babak Taghvaee)

F-5F 3-7181 was one of the last few aircraft of this variant built for Iran. After being stored for many years due to a lack of spares, it was recently overhauled by the IRIAF at Mehrabad and returned to service.
(Babak Taghvaee)

75

IRIAF 2010

Most 41st TFS F-5Es now wear this new 'warpaint', showing a bald eagle. This was introduced in October 2009 with the intention of boosting the morale of young pilots assigned to the unit.
(Babak Taghvaee)

The 43rd TFS nickname is 'The Tigers' and all the unit's F-5Es now wear tiger insignia on the starboard side of their fin.
(Babak Taghvaee)

TFB.4 Vahdati

A row of F-5Fs on the tarmac at TFB.4. Note the fin of F-5F 3-7155, showing the eagle insignia that has been worn on the port side of the fin of most 41st TFS F-5Es since 2009. (Babak Taghvaee)

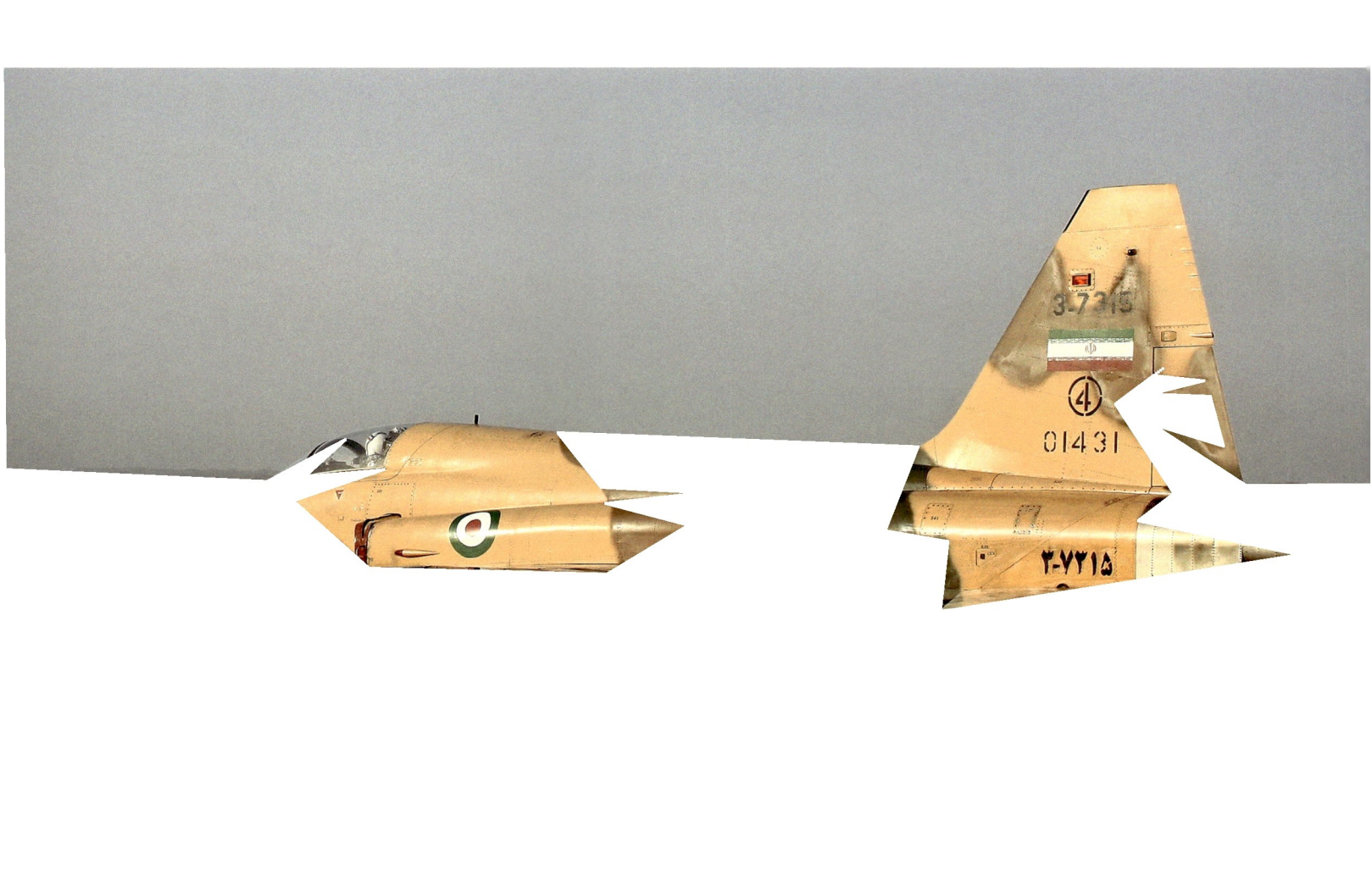

F-5E 3-7315 is the former 3-7140 (USAF 74-01431 and c/n U1128). During the 1990s, this aircraft saw extensive service in the course of testing installations for Chinese-made PL-7 and Russian-made R-60MK air-to-air missiles, in the process of which IRIAF engineers designed corresponding wingtip launch rails. (Babak Taghvaee)

TFB.4 Vahdati

A row of F-5s at TFB.4 in early 2009. F-5F 3-7155 (USAF 75-0682; foreground, right) was only the second aircraft of this variant built for Iran. It served with the 41st TFS from 1976 until 2009, when it was reassigned to the 43rd TFS.
(IRIAF)

F-5E 3-7330 is one of the examples modified under Project Azarakhsh, launched in the 1990s by HESA with the intention of upgrading the aircraft's fire-control system, other avionics and armament.
(Babak Taghvaee)

F-5E 3-7301 (left) and F-5F Azaraksh 3-7176 (right) roll for take-off prior to the military parade over Tehran on 22 September 2009.
(Babak Taghvaee)

Tactical Fighter Base 5   Ardestani

The prospective Omidiyeh 11th Tactical Fighter Base, under construction near Ahvaz, became the last air base to be built during the IIAF era. Envisaged as a very modern facility to operate F-5E/F and F-16A/B jets, this installation was designed with some assistance from Israel. By 1977 construction of Omidiyeh was only around 50 per cent complete, and although originally envisaged to be operational by 1978, reduced priority saw this date slip to as late as 1981.

Omidiyeh – the designation of which at some stage was changed to TFB.5 – was to provide sufficient infrastructure to accommodate three fighter squadrons. The 1979 Revolution practically put an end to the development of TFB.5, leaving only 12 of the first 20 hardened aircraft shelters complete. No administrative buildings, maintenance facilities or housing were yet in place. Similarly, the process of establishing three F-5E/F units – all planned to eventually convert to the F-16 – was stopped. Following the cancellation of Iran's massive F-16 project, most of the F-5s that were planned to enter service with units to be based at TFB.5 were handed over to squadrons at TFB.2 and TFB.4.

Some construction work on TFB.5 restarted in 1979, when two alert shelters and some other installations were finished. Omidiyeh was all but complete when the war with Iraq began, with all major facilities erected, with the exception of housing and various support facilities. Due to its proximity to the war fronts, the facility was used as a hub for the transport aircraft that brought in reinforcements and supplies from other parts of Iran, and it repeatedly hosted temporary deployments of combat aircraft.

During the early phases of the war, the IRIAF personnel stationed at Omidiyeh had to sleep in tents, but by 1982 some housing facilities had been constructed. By 1986 the airfield had expanded sufficiently enough for the IRGC to consider about taking it over from the air force. Such plans were never realised, however, and the IRIAF instead housed its new Chinese-made F-7N point-defence fighters there.

TFB.5 was re-named Ardestani AB after Mostafa Ardestani, a war hero F-5 pilot who was killed in an aircraft crash in January 1995. He was also the only Iranian pilot ever to fly a MiG-25.

Since 2007, the IRGC has been exercising increasing pressure on the IRIAF to hand over TFB.5. In reaction, the air force developed plans to redeploy Ardestani's units either to TFB.14, or a new air base under construction west of Birjand. Although this project appears to have been cancelled, the future of TFB.5 currently remains uncertain.

51st, 52nd and 53rd Tactical Fighter Squadrons

Plans were drawn up in the late 1970s to form three units equipped with F-5E/Fs and to be based at Ardestani. Following the completion of the associated crew training, by 1980 all three were to convert to the F-16A/B. Again, most of the corresponding plans were cancelled due to the Revolution, but there are several reports indicating that at least some of the three squadrons might have been established and declared operational well before that date.

The only certainty is that the unit designations reappeared when Iran concluded a deal with China in July 1986 covering the delivery of as many as 140 F-7N and FT-7N fighters. During the same year the first 15 F-7Ns and 5 FT-7Ns arrived at TFB.8 on board several transport aircraft that reached Iran via Pakistan. These jets were originally intended for the IRGC's air arm – by then renamed as an 'air force'. Upon their arrival in Iran, the F-7s were assembled and test-flown by the Chinese. Meanwhile, another group of Chinese engineers oversaw construction of maintenance hangars and some other associated facilities at TFB.5.

The F-7 is an export variant of the Chinese copy of the venerable Mikoyan i Gurevich MiG-21F-13 interceptor. Sometimes marketed under the name Airguard, it is armed with two 30mm cannon, and can be equipped with the Chinese-made PL-7 air-to-air missile (a copy of the French Matra R.550 Magic).

However, in Iranian service the type soon became known as nothing less than a maintenance nightmare. The hydraulic and pneumatic systems proved unreliable, while the poor engine manufacturing quality also caused several near-fatal accidents. Eventually, the IRGC discarded the F-7 and handed all the aircraft over to the IRIAF. In order to train the required new group of IRIAF pilots and maintainers, the type entered service with the 51st TFS only several months after the end of the war with Iraq, in 1988.

Despite countless problems experienced when introducing the F-7 to service, during the late 1980s the IRIAF was so starved of operational combat aircraft that a decision was made to continue the acquisition process. In 1990, a second batch of F-7Ns and FT-7Ns – a total of 40 aircraft – was delivered to TFB.8. Once again assembled with the help of Chinese engineers, most of these aircraft entered service with the newly established 52nd and 53rd TFS, while half of the delivered FT-7Ns were taken up by the newly established 85th TFS (for details of this unit, see the section on TFB.8).

By early 1992 the IRIAF was able to declare three units equipped with F-7Ns operational at TFB.5: the 51st, 52nd and 53rd TFS. Poor manufacturing quality of the Chinese-built aircraft remains an issue today. The F-7 is colloquially known as the 'Flying Kettle' within the IRIAF, and Iran eventually decided to cancel any further procurement of the type, together with most of the projects that were planned to be realised with Chinese assistance during the mid-1990s.

IRGC pressure on the IRIAF to hand over control of TFB.5 has forced the air force to contemplate relocation of the 51st, 52nd and 53rd TFS to a new air base in eastern Iran. This latter facility has been under construction some 150km west of Birjand since 2007. Although all three squadrons remained operational at TFB.5 as of early 2010, their fate and possible future designations are currently uncertain.

TFB.5 Ardestani

Recognising the limited abilities of its F-7 fleet, the IRIAF began reorienting the units flying this type to air-to-ground roles. Correspondingly, a new camouflage pattern was applied on aircraft passing through periodic overhaul at Mehrabad, this closely resembling that worn by IRIAF F-5s.
(Babak Taghvaee)

While originally delivered in an air-superiority camouflage, the FT-7Ms of TFB.5 are now increasingly adopting the same camouflage pattern as the F-7M and F-5E/F. Notable is the internal 23mm gun installed in this Chinese-made aircraft, not available on Soviet/Russian-built two-seat variants of MiG-21.
(Babak Taghvaee)

As originally delivered to Iran, all F-7Ms were painted in this air superiority camouflage pattern and primarily served as point-defence interceptors. Although they retain such capabilities, more recently the fleet has been primarily used for air-to-ground purposes, which explains the unguided rocket pods displayed with this aircraft.
(Liam F. Devlin)

Iran's F-7M variant differs in several details compared to F-7s delivered to other countries. While most equipment is Chinese-manufactured, the IRIAF's aircraft carry plenty of Western avionics and are compatible with a range of US-designed weapons.
(Liam F. Devlin)

Tactical Fighter Base 6   Yassini

The Bushehr 6th Tactical Fighter Base (TFB.6) was constructed on a fertile peninsula southwest of the port city of Bushehr in the early 1970s. Mainly built with US assistance, some advice was also provided by Israel. Construction of the facility was the result of a requirement by the Shah and the IIAF for a major air base that could protect the strategically important oil-exporting facilities on Kharg Island, as well as Iranian interests in the northern Persian Gulf.

In 1973, as soon as the necessary installations were complete, the IIAF began the work of establishing three units – the 61st, 62nd and 63rd TFS – each equipped with 16 F-4Es.

The beginning of operations at Bushehr was followed by the construction of a major early warning radar station equipped with the most modern US-made radar systems north of Bushehr. This was complemented by several SAM and anti-aircraft artillery sites.

Early on in the Iran-Iraq War, TFB.6 came under sporadic attacks from the Iraqi Air Force. As expected, the 'Bushehri' squadrons responded in kind, bombing several key Iraqi air bases and oil installations in the south. The Bushehri Phantoms also effectively prevented the Iraqi Navy from venturing anywhere inside the Persian Gulf for most of the eight-year war. Together with TFB.3 and TFB.4, fighter-bombers from Bushehr flew thousands of combat sorties over Iraq as well as the battlefields of southwest Iran.

In 1985, TFB.6 was reinforced through the forward deployment of an F-14 interceptor squadron from TFB.8. Despite an interruption in Tomcat operations from Bushehr between 2002 and 2008, detachments of F-14s are once again being rotated through TFB.6.

Meanwhile, maintenance facilities at TFB.6 have been expanded in order to begin overhauling both F-4Es and F-14s. The first locally overhauled Phantom, belonging to the 61st TFS, was rolled out in April 2009.

61st Tactical Fighter Squadron

The pace of operations at TFB.6 has been very high ever since the air base and its three constituent Phantom squadrons were established. During most of the 1970s, Phantoms flew on average 20 CAP and training sorties each day, with pilots averaging between 260 and 300 flight hours a year. At least four F-4Es were held on permanent alert, armed with two AIM-7E Sparrow and four AIM-9P Sidewinder air-to-air missiles, as well as AN/ALQ-119 ECM pods.

The base also hosted some 11th TRS RF-4 operations, these flying reconnaissance missions over the entire Persian Gulf region during the 1970s.

As expected, the situation changed dramatically following the Revolution of 1979, but particularly from June 1980, after the failed Nojeh coup attempt and amid other political tensions. Many officers and pilots based at TFB.6 were arrested or forced into early retirement, and in common with several other IRIAF air bases, Bushehr subsequently experienced severe shortages of qualified personnel and low operability of its aircraft. Flying and training almost ground to a halt in the following months, and only a handful of F-4Es remained in operational condition.

Nevertheless, TFB.6 was only the second IRIAF air base to react to the Iraqi invasion. Barely two hours after the opening Iraqi air raids, four F-4Es from Bushehr bombed targets in southern Iraq, and on the following morning 20 F-4Es from TFB.6 participated in the 140-aircraft raid deep into Iraq.

During the following eight years of fighting, Phantoms from TFB.6 took part in most of the operations against Iraq. They caused major damage to the Iraqi Navy, and flew critically important protection missions for merchant shipping convoys moving supplies to the Iranian ports of Bandar Khomeini and Mahshahr in Khowr Musa in the northern Persian Gulf.

The Bushehr F-4s also flew thousands of CAPs over Kharg Island, and supported ground operations on the front lines around Abadan and Khoramshahr, as well as the Basra and Faw areas inside Iraq. Between 1981 and 1983 pilots from Bushehr distinguished themselves in air combat against a growing number of increasingly sophisticated Iraqi interceptors, downing a number of Mikoyan i Gurevich MiG-23s and Mirage F.1EQs. These were sometimes downed in conventional dogfights, but the F-4s often fought with air-to-air missiles over ranges well beyond 20km.

Later on in the war, Bushehr Phantoms became involved in the so-called 'Tanker War' together with their compatriots from Bandar Abbas. This brought them on a collision course with the Royal Saudi Air Force (RSAF), resulting in several air combats – and losses – against the superior McDonnell Douglas F-15C Eagles in 1984.

One of most famous Iranian F-4E pilots of the war, Captain Ali-Reza Yassini was responsible for sinking or damaging several Iraqi naval vessels in the course of Operation Morvarid in late November 1980. He flew many of his combat sorties from this air base, before he became deputy commander of TFB.3. The Bushehr base was named after him following his death in an aircraft accident in January 1995.

By the end of the war with Iraq, the number of F-4Es at TFB.6 had declined to such a degree that all the remaining F-4Es and their crews from the three units were merged into the 61st TFS.

In 2008, pending completion of the works on the first Bushehr-overhauled F-4E, and considering the unit's proud combat heritage, the commanding officer of the 61st TFS received permission from IRIAF High Command to paint sharkmouths on all his Phantoms. The first F-4E to wear the new insignia was 3-6548, rolled out in April 2009. By the following year, most of the Bushehr-based Phantoms were wearing sharkmouths.

Nowadays the 61st TFS F-4Es have returned to flying their routine CAPs and training sorties over the Persian Gulf. They also undertake regular dissimilar training with F-5E/Fs from TFB.4 and F-7s from TFB.5, and sometimes deploy to these air bases. At least two Phantoms are meanwhile held on permanent alert at Bushehr.

63rd Tactical Fighter Squadron

The original 63rd TFS came into being as an F-4E unit in 1973–74. Following the end of the war with Iraq, the remaining crews and aircraft of this unit – together with those from the 62nd TFS – were reassigned to the 61st TFS. Nevertheless, a new 63rd TFS came into being only some time later, when the 83rd TFS F-14 detachment that had been forward deployed to TFB.6 since 1985 was re-designated as a squadron.

The 63rd TFS was again disbanded in 2002, when it was decided to move its aircraft and crews back to Esfahan. Nevertheless, in the face of increasing tensions with Israel and the US, and in order to protect the first Iranian nuclear reactors in Bushehr, the IRIAF re-established the F-14 presence at Bushehr through the deployment of Tomcats from the 83rd TFS, a unit that continues the traditions of the 63rd TFS. Ever since, at least two Tomcats have been held on permanent alert at Bushehr.

TFB.6 Yassini

Two 'sharks of Bushehr' on a training sortie north of their base, in early 2010. The F-4E remains the backbone of the IRIAF and investments have not only ensured the fleet remains operational but have also resulted in a number of upgrades and modifications.
(Bravo Alpha via F. Shamas/Iranian Aviation Review)

One of the 'sharks of Bushehr' – an IRIAF F-4 unit with particularly proud traditions of combat service during the war with Iraq. (Bravo Alpha via F. Shamas/Iranian Aviation Review)

TFB.6 Yassini

Illustrating the F-4E's massive load-carrying capability, this Phantom from TFB.6 displays a warload of no less than 24 locally assembled Mk 82-type training bombs.
(Bravo Alpha via F. Shamas/Iranian Aviation Review)

When new maintenance facilities were established at TFB.6, and F-4Es of the 61st TFS began to be regularly maintained there, the commanding officer of this unit requested permission from IRIAF High Command for his aircraft to be decorated with sharkmouth insignia. Permission was granted and most of the Phantoms based at Yassini AB are now decorated in this fashion.
(Babak Taghvaee)

IRIAF 2010

TFB.6 Yassini

IRIAF 2010

Photographs of the first IRIAF F-4E decorated with the sharkmouth marking appeared in spring 2009, to the considerable surprise of Western observers. (Babak Taghvaee)

A sharkmouth-decorated F-4E launches from TFB.6 in early 2010. (Babak Taghvaee) ◄

Tactical Fighter Base 7   Dowran

In the late 1960s the IIAF was searching for a site where another 'strategic' air base could be constructed as a home for a fleet of potent fighter-bombers that it intended to acquire in response to deliveries of Tupolev Tu-16 bombers to Iraq. Initially, the IIAF wanted General Dynamics F-111 bombers, but when the Americans turned down this request, Iran instead opted for the McDonnell Douglas F-4D Phantom II.

As soon as a contract for the acquisition of 32 F-4Ds had been signed in July 1967, construction work began at Shiraz. Originally designated as the 4th Tactical Fighter Base (TFB.4), this huge installation was declared operational in September 1968. It initially included six dual hardened aircraft shelters for F-4Ds, constructed in the northwest corner of the facility, with nine other hardened shelters in the southwest corner.

Three additional shelters were subsequently constructed on the western side, for the purpose of protecting the alert aircraft. Eventually, a very large ramp was built in the centre of the northern side, once it had been decided to base the majority of the IIAF transport fleet here.

The first F-4Ds and C-130s arrived at TFB.4 in 1968, entering service with the 401st and 402nd TFS, and with the 2nd Transport Wing, respectively. Within the following five years, the IIAF issued three successive orders for F-4Es, and the intake of such a number of Phantoms prompted a major re-organisation of not only Shiraz, but also the entire air force. This became effective in January 1974, and saw TFB.4 re-designated as the Tactical Fighter Base 7 (TFB.7).

The pace of new arrivals and changes increased in subsequent years. Both the F-4D units were re-designated in 1974, and by 1976 one of them had been re-equipped with F-4Es. Also receiving F-4Es was a new, third Phantom squadron at TFB.7, which by then was named Taddayon AB. Barely a year later, both the F-4E units were again re-equipped, this time with no fewer than 30 F-14As.

Meanwhile, the 2nd Transport Wing was re-designated as the 72nd TFW, and was expanded to include two units flying C-130s. As additional facilities and aircraft became available, through the mid-1970s the TFB.7 also became home to a SAR Squadron (originally flying HH-43Fs, and later Bell 214Cs). Correspondingly, by 1978 the composition of the locally based units was as provided in Table 3.

Following the Revolution, personnel at TFB.7, which was by now – unofficially – renamed as Horr AB, did their best to keep themselves, their base and their equipment in operational condition. Nevertheless, massive cuts in the defence budget grounded the majority of its aircraft, and local units also lost a number of personnel following the Nojeh coup attempt. By the time of the Iraqi invasion on 22 September 1980, only 12 F-5Es 'borrowed' from TFB.10 took part in the 140-aircraft raid against Iraq the next morning. Meanwhile, locally based F-4Ds and F-14s only joined the fray in the following days. A number of F-4Ds were also deployed to TFB.4 to conduct interdiction missions into Iraq.

Table 3: IIAF units based at TFB.7, 1978

Unit designation	Aircraft type	Remarks
71st TFS	14 x F-4D	Nicknamed 'Sharpshooters'
72nd TFS	15 x F-14A	
73rd TFS	15 x F-14A	
71st TAS	12 x C-130E/H	
72nd TAS	12 x C-130E/H	
SAR Squadron	4 x Bell 214C	

In autumn 1980, TFB.7 again saw a number of reorganisations and redeployments. Most of its F-4Ds were redeployed to TFB.4, while several F-14As were attached to TFB.1, to fly constant CAPs over the Iranian capital. On the other hand, TFB.7 became the main base for the Lockheed P-3F Orion maritime patrol aircraft squadron, which arrived from TFB.9.

The F-4Ds from TFB.7 undertook frequent deployments in the course of the early IRIAF offensives against Iraq. Flown by some of the youngest but also the bravest crews, they deployed laser-guided bombs against targets including bridges. However, they were exposed to all types of Iraqi air defences, and suffered exceptionally heavy losses within the first weeks of fighting. Correspondingly, the use of laser-guided bombs was discontinued, and the remaining aircraft reverted to more 'conventional' munitions.

In 1985, in the light of attacks on Tehran by the Iraqi Air Force's Mach 3-capable MiG-25 fighter-bombers, and due to increasing maintenance and spare parts management issues, all the remaining F-14s were concentrated at TFB.8. Almost simultaneously, the remaining F-4Ds were also handed over to TFB.10, and were replaced by F-5As and RF-5As.

In June 1989, Iran signed a major defence contract with the USSR, which included an order for 12 Sukhoi Su-24MK bombers. The IRIAF had originally envisaged acquisition of up to 100 aircraft of this type, and set in motion an effort to expand the existing facilities at TFB.7 in order to base most of its new Su-24s there.

However, lack of funding as well as US pressure on Moscow forced the IRIAF to settle on a much smaller fleet. This fleet was initially based at TFB.1, with only nine new shelters having been constructed at TFB.7 by 1995. Only the evacuation of 24 Su-24MKs from Iraq in January and February 1991 eventually enabled the IRIAF to establish two new units equipped with the type. In 1996 both of these moved to TFB.7, replacing the remaining F-5As and RF-5As of the 71st TFS.

Later in the 1990s TFB.7 was officially renamed as Dowran AB, in memory of a renowned F-4E pilot killed during the war with Iraq.

71st Tactical Fighter Squadron

The 71st TFS was originally established as the 401st TFS in September 1968, in order to fly the first 16 F-4Ds acquired by Iran. Suffering attrition of up to nine Phantoms in peacetime accidents by 1974, the unit was re-designated as the 71st TFS, and two years later merged with the 72nd TFS to form a new 71st TFS, nicknamed the 'Sharpshooters'.

During the late 1970s, the IIAF launched Project Peace Enforcer, part of which was to see 14 F-4Ds equipped with advanced radar homing and warning (RHAW) systems that would enable them to locate enemy air defences and act as pathfinders for other Phantoms in strike packages. Although all the required equipment was purchased and delivered, only eight F-4Ds received the corresponding modifications before the 1979 Revolution. Of the modified aircraft, five were lost during the first week of the war with Iraq.

Although the attrition rates of Iranian F-4Ds decreased in subsequent years, and despite the considerable success achieved by their crews – particularly in aerial combat with Iraqi fighter-bombers – by 1985 the number of remaining F-4Ds had decreased to such a degree that they had to be withdrawn from combat and assigned to a training role. They were therefore handed over to TFB.10 and the 71st TFS was re-equipped with the remaining F-5As and RF-5As of the 11th TRS, as well as a number of F-5As and F-5Es acquired from Ethiopia. Further-

Table 4: IRIAF units based at TFB.7, 2010

Unit designation	Aircraft type	Remarks
71st TFS	Su-24MK	
72nd TAS	C-130E/H and Il-76MD/TD	
71st ASW Squadron	P-3F	
SAR Squadron	Bell 214C	

more, given that the IRIAF needed new pilots, this squadron was designated as the IRIAF's Advanced and Weapons Training Squadron, and during the late 1980s was further reinforced through the addition of several F-5As obtained from Vietnam.

Although flying the Su-24 for two decades, the 71st TFS still lacks sufficient numbers of hardened aircraft shelters to house all of its 12 aircraft. This results in the aircraft spending most of their time parked on the apron on the southwest side of TFB.7 and exposed to the elements, in turn increasing their maintenance requirements.

72nd Tactical Fighter Squadron

This unit came into being as the 402nd TFS, which was established in September 1969 to operate the second batch of 16 F-4Ds purchased from the US. In 1974 it was re-designated as the 72nd TFS, and two years later re-equipped with F-4Es while assisting in the establishment of the third Phantom squadron at TFB.7, the 73rd TFS. Another major reorganisation followed in 1977, when the 72nd and 73rd TFS converted to the F-14.

The 72nd and 73rd TFS flew Tomcats until the end of the Iran-Iraq War, when all the remaining airframes were concentrated at TFB.8, and both units disbanded, pending deliveries of Su-24MKs from the USSR. Deliveries of this type and crew training began in 1990, and intensified in the following two years.

However, the Su-24 did not prove easy to master and many of the older pilots, trained in the US, experienced considerable problems adjusting to an aircraft with instruments that used the metric system. Unsurprisingly, peacetime attrition was considerable, with five Su-24MKs being written off in various accidents during the 1990s. The worst of these saw a Su-24 collide with an Iran Air Tours Tupolev Tu-154M over Mehrabad on 8 February 1993, killing all 133 passengers and crewmembers onboard the airliner and the Sukhoi aircraft.

The 72nd TFS continued operating the Su-24 into the early years of the 21st century, until the number of operational airframes fell to a level where the unit had to be merged into the 71st TFS, and the squadron was disbanded.

72nd Transport Air Squadron

Between 1969 and 1974, the IIAF established two squadrons equipped with C-130E/H transports and based them at TFB.7. These were the 71st and 72nd TAS. Both units served with great distinction during the war with Iraq, flying thousands of sorties while hauling reinforcements and supplies from all over the country to the battlefields. The fleet was eventually worn out to such a degree that in 1992 the two units had to be merged into a single unit that retained the 72nd TAS designation.

Previously, the unit had been reinforced through the receipt of nine Ilyushin Il-76MD and Il-76TD heavy transports evacuated from Iraq in 1991. Following their refurbishment at Mehrabad with the help of locally manufactured spare parts, the Ilyushins entered service with the 72nd TAS. The unit therefore became a unique transport asset since it operated aircraft of both US and Soviet/Russian origin. The squadron still retains at least one aircraft of each type on permanent alert for deployment in emergency situations.

During the 1990s, sizeable maintenance facilities were established for the squadron at TFB.7, including a C-130 hangar on the northwest side of Shiraz airport (west of the 72nd TAS ramp). The disused F-4 and F-14 hardened aircraft shelters were meanwhile used as administrative facilities as well as for storage depots and maintenance workshops. The same area is often used to park Il-76s that lack spare parts or are awaiting overhaul.

71st Anti-Submarine Warfare Squadron

In order to obtain an advanced sea control and anti-submarine warfare capability, in 1973 the IIAF ordered a total of six P-3F Orion maritime patrol aircraft. The variant in question used the airframe of the well-known P-3C variant, with some equipment from the earlier P-3A and P-3B models. Prior to the Revolution, the IIAF had planned to eventually arm all of its Orions with the McDonnell Douglas AGM-84A Harpoon anti-ship missile, although only one aircraft was modified accordingly before 1979, and this was lost in a fatal accident in 1985.

Orion deliveries to Iran commenced in April 1975, with the intention of the IIAF managing the training of their aircrew and maintainers, before handing over the entire fleet to Imperial Iranian Naval Aviation (IINA). The fleet was initially based at Bandar Abbas TFMB.9 (see the corresponding section below), and was operated by the 91st ASW Squadron. Following the Iraqi invasion it was moved to the more secure and isolated TFB.7 in 1980, where the facilities of the then two resident C-130 units were assigned to the newly re-designated 71st ASW Squadron.

During the war, the IRIAF P-3Fs saw extensive service, and mainly operated over the lower Persian Gulf, the Strait of Hormuz and the Gulf of Oman, ensuring the security of international merchant shipping and tankers in this crucial part of the world. At the same time they also encountered foreign – primarily US Navy – warships and aircraft on a regular basis.

By the 1990s the P-3Fs were in a relatively poor condition, prompting the then C-in-C of the IRIAF to request additional funding for maintenance directly from the Iranian leadership, without success. The unit experienced another crisis several years ago, when most of its personnel reached their retirement age. Although the government again refused to increase funding for the 71st ASW Squadron, the IRIAF eventually found the required finances by cancelling other projects. Subsequently, the remaining five Orions were overhauled and new crews were trained. Nevertheless, there is no doubt that the IRIAF urgently needs a new maritime patrol aircraft.

Liaison Squadron (or 'PC-6 Squadron')

In 1983 and 1984, the IRIAF purchased 15 Pilatus PC-6B2-H2 light transport aircraft from Switzerland. Powered by the Garrett PT6A-27 engine and in possession of excellent handling and take-off and landing performance, the PC-6s entered service with a newly established Light Transport Squadron based at Dowshan Tappeh AB. Originally serving in the liaison role, they also saw deployment for SAR duties, several times flying deep into Iraq to pick up downed IRIAF airmen.

In the early 1990s, two PC-6s were temporarily loaned to the Postal Service's Payam, an airline specialised in postal transport, but both aircraft were taken back by the IRIAF when Payam managed to acquire four Embraer EMB-110P-1s. In the mid-1990s, the squadron operating the remaining PC-6s moved to TFB.7, and most of the aircraft received an overhaul and new, 'civilian-style' liveries. Although not very often seen in public in recent years, the PC-6 squadron is still operational. The unit resides on the eastern part of TFB.7's ramp, which is also occupied by the 71st ASW Squadron.

Dowran SAR Squadron

The first SAR unit permanently assigned to Shiraz airport was established in 1968, and was equipped with seven HH-43F helicopters. In 1977, the Huskies were replaced by four newly built Bell 214Cs. Although based relatively far from the border with Iraq, the TFB.7 SAR squadron saw combat deployments along the battlefields during the war, and even lost several helicopters to ground fire. Due to attrition, the number of available airframes decreased, and in the 1990s the IRIAF was forced to concentrate the entire remaining fleet of Bell 214Cs within two units, based at TFB.1 and TFB.7, respectively. All remaining helicopters of this type were subsequently overhauled at the HESA facility at Shahin-Shahr, and three were still operational at the Dowran air base as of 2010.

Su-24MK 3-6809 on finals at Mehrabad AB, carrying a UPAZ-1A refuelling pod. IRIAF Su-24 crews fly frequent and intensive in-flight refuelling operations. (Babak Taghvaee) ▶▶

TFB.7 Dowran

Su-24MK 3-6807 is a one of several survivors from the original batch of 12 aircraft purchased directly from the former USSR in 1989. Contrary to the former Iraqi aircraft operated by the 71st TFS, it has wing fences containing chaff and flare dispensers.
(Babak Taghvaee)

The Su-24MK remains the most potent strike platform in IRIAF service. This ex-Iraqi example displays the camouflage pattern that is now standard across most of the fleet, including examples delivered from the USSR.
(Babak Taghvaee)

IRIAF 2010

TFB.7 Dowran

Su-24MK 3-6843 on display in early 2010. The weapons system of the type has been considerably upgraded, making the Su-24 compatible with a range of US- and Chinese-designed weaponry. The aircraft is also capable of refuelling from the US-made Beech 1800 pods carried by Boeing 707 tankers.
(Babak Taghvaee)

Previously, their revised camouflage pattern made ex-Iraqi Su-24MKs distinguishable from Soviet deliveries. Today, this is not always the case – Su-24MK 3-6809 was acquired from the former USSR but received the new camouflage pattern during overhaul by IACI.
(Babak Taghvaee)

TFB.7 Dowran

Most Il-76s in service with the 72nd TAS comprise 11 aircraft of this type flown to Iran from Iraq in January 1991. Some of them have since received a camouflage pattern, while this example wears an attractive white, green and grey livery.
(Babak Taghvaee)

A study showing the details of the nose section of Il-76TD 5-8203.
(Babak Taghvaee)

IRIAF 2010

TFB.7 Dowran

5-8204

Another view of 5-8204 on finals at Mehrabad AB. The IRIAF Il-76 fleet is gradually approaching a point at which it will require complete overhaul in order to remain operational.
(Babak Taghvaee)

C-130E (or H) 5-8520 is one of most mysterious Hercules in IRIAF service. A C-130 wearing this serial number crashed on 19 June 1979 near Shiraz when operated by the 71st TAS. Where the replacement aircraft came from is unknown, but likely sources include Pakistan and Vietnam.
(Babak Taghvaee)

TFB.7 Dowran

Il-76s of the 72nd TAS are heavily utilised, moving IRIAF personnel and equipment, as well as supporting various other branches, and operating in support of relief operations for the frequent earthquakes in Iran. It is therefore hardly surprising that the camouflage pattern of this example (5-8209) is so worn out.
(Babak Taghvaee)

IRIAF Il-76TD 5-8204 prepares to land at Mehrabad AB. Although the road network in Iran has been significantly improved over the last 40 years, the IRIAF is still heavily dependent on the services of its transport aircraft – particularly faster jets like the Il-76.
(Babak Taghvaee) ◄◄

IRIAF 2010

One of several C-130E/Hs still in service with the 72nd TAS, a unit that operates both jet- and turboprop-powered transport aircraft. (Babak Taghvaee)

TFB.7 Dowran

Against all odds and in the face of countless reports of its withdrawal, the small fleet of P-3F maritime patrol aircraft remains operational with the 71st Anti-Submarine Warfare Squadron, based at TFB.7.
(Ali Reza)

P-3F 5-8704 on finals at TFB.7. Note the official IRIAF crest applied behind the cockpit.
(Ali Reza) ▶

107

IRIAF 2010

TFB.7 Dowran

The little-known, small fleet of Pilatus PC-6B light transports operated by the IRIAF from the mid-1980s were in storage for several years. Recently, a few aircraft have been returned to service and the squadron flying them is operational again.
(Babak Taghvaee)

One of several Bell 214Cs operated by the Dowran SAR Squadron.
(Babak Taghvaee)

Tactical Fighter Base 8   Baba'i

Construction of the future 8th Tactical Fighter Base (TFB.8) was originally based on plans for the establishment of a second IIAF 'strategic' air base, located in the desert near the city of Esfahan, in central Iran. Eventually, this air base evolved into the centre of operations for Iran's F-14A Tomcat interceptor fleet, as part of Project Persian King, launched in January 1974.

Designed using what were then most advanced ideas, the base received two lengthy runways, each wide enough to enable simultaneous take-off by up to three F-14s, or to accept wide-body transports like the IIAF's Boeing 747s. Since the air force eventually intended to purchase more than 150 F-14s, over time up to 50 double hardened aircraft shelters were constructed, sufficient to shelter 100 Tomcats, along with extensive maintenance and storage facilities, a large accommodation complex and a number of multi-storey administrative buildings. Finally, during the 1970s, a full battalion of MIM-23B I-HAWK SAMs protected TFB.8, with several missile batteries positioned on the hills overlooking the vast facility, supported by dozens of anti-aircraft gun positions.

Deliveries of the Tomcat to Iran began in January 1976, by which time the first group of IIAF pilots had also completed their training, and Khatami TFB.8, named after the popular IIAF commander who was killed in a hang-gliding accident in September 1975, was officially declared operational. With extensive help from Grumman Aerospace Corporation and US military advisers, within the following two years three squadrons equipped with the F-14 became operational, while the Americans installed most of the maintenance facilities that had also been purchased by the IIAF.

Meanwhile, the air force began preparations for acquisition of 160 to 300 F-16A/Bs. In consideration of this order, the idea emerged to further expand TFB.8. This was to be achieved through the construction of two additional runways and another huge complex of shelters on the southern side of the airfield, where an entire F-16 wing could be stationed. All such plans were axed, however, following the 1979 Revolution. Plans for establishing extensive training facilities at TFB.8 were also abandoned.

Immediately after coming to power, the new government, stunned by the excessive cost of operating the F-14, expressed its wish to sell all its Tomcats either back to the US, or to Canada, the UK or Saudi Arabia. Pending a decision on this matter, most of the fleet was grounded and stored. Given that most of the officers involved in Project Persian King spent years training in the US, with a few even undergoing specialist courses in Israel, their loyalty to the new the authorities was questioned. A sizeable group of pilots and ground personnel was therefore forced to leave the service, and soon the IRIAF faced shortages of qualified manpower capable of maintaining its Tomcats. Nevertheless, negotiations over the possible re-sale of the F-14s stalled in the face of domestic opposition and increasing tensions between Iran and the US. Having been recognised as crucial elements in the defence of Iranian airspace, therefore, the type remained in service, although by summer 1980 only 12 F-14As remained in operational condition.

Immediately prior to and following the start of the war with Iraq, the IRIAF was ordered to increase its readiness levels, and TFB.8 scrambled to return as many F-14s to service as possible. As the number of available and operational aircraft increased through October 1980, their role in preventing the Iraqi Air Force from operating freely within Iranian airspace became ever more crucial. By the end of the year, Tomcat crews from TFB.8 had claimed up to 40 aerial victories against Iraqi aircraft.

Between 1981 and 1983, the F-14 squadrons from Esfahan were involved in a major battle for air superiority over the Khuzestan province in southwest Iran. In the course of this fighting they remained successful even though they faced Iraq's ever more advanced fighters of French and Soviet origin. In the process of downing more than a dozen Mirages and MiGs, only two F-14s were damaged in air combat. Realising that it had been involved in a war of attrition with no end in sight, and that there was no possibility of buying any attrition replacement aircraft (particularly not in the class of the Tomcat), from 1984 the IRIAF moved its focus away from the battle over Khuzestan.

Instead, the air force concentrated on protecting the areas of vital interest to Iran, foremost the oil facilities on and around Kharg Island, the capital city, and shipping convoys heading to or from Iranian ports and oil terminals in the northern and central Persian Gulf.

By the end of the war, aircraft from TFB.8 had claimed over 80 victories against Iraqi aircraft, many of them within the last eight months of the conflict, when they became involved in a series of extensive air battles over the Persian Gulf. In total, seven F-14s had been lost by July 1988, including four shot down by the Iraqis, two shot down by Iranian air defences, and one lost to engine failure. At least six other F-14s were badly damaged, while 30 others were grounded due to a lack of spares. The grounded aircraft were largely cannibalised to keep the rest of the fleet operational.

The number of pilots available to all three F-14 units based at TFB.8 decreased through combat attrition, fatigue and health problems caused by intensive flying throughout the long war, together with reassignments to other posts and emigration. As a result, in late 1984 and early 1985 it was decided to convert a number of pilots flying other types in IRIAF service to the Tomcat. This effort was one of the reasons that prompted the IRIAF to begin establishing an Air Force Academy, including all the necessary training installations, at TFB.8.

The base itself was now renamed Baba'i AB, in memory of a leading Iranian F-14 pilot and military commander. In the course of the subsequent reorganisation of local units, all the remaining F-14s from TFB.7 were reassigned to the units based at TFB.8, although one Tomcat squadron then moved to TFB.6 on a more permanent basis. At the same time, TFB.8 received various training aircraft – including the entire fleet of Pilatus PC-7s purchased from Switzerland, as well as a sizeable number of T-33s, F-5A/Bs and FT-7s – to serve with units assigned to the Air Force Academy.

Until 2004, the IRIAF F-14 fleet and thus the entire TFB.8 support effort languished on the edge of remaining operational. However, thanks foremost to the relentless efforts of the late Gen Abbas Hazin, himself an active F-14 pilot with plenty of experience from the war with Iraq, a major revitalisation project was launched. This resulted in the reactivation and return to service of most of the surviving Tomcat fleet. As of 2010, the F-14 Tomcat remains the backbone of the Iranian interceptor fleet, and TFB.8 is the type's major base.

81st, 82nd and 83rd Tactical Fighter Squadrons

The 81st, 82nd and 83rd TFS came into being between mid-January 1976 and February 1978, in order to operate the F-14 Tomcats based at TFB.8. Apart from losing a number of early Tomcat pilots who quit the service or were purged, all three units remained intact – and well protected – during the Revolution, the Nojeh coup attempt and the border skirmishes prior to the Iraqi invasion.

However, most of their aircraft were stored and were therefore inactive. As the number of operational F-14s increased during late 1980 and 1981, however, some differences of opinion emerged on how 'loyal' the authorities considered their crews, as well as their combat effectiveness. While the 81st TFS distinguished itself early on in the conflict, the 82nd TFS gradually became – and remained – the most successful IRIAF Tomcat squadron of the war, despite the fact that a number of pilots assigned to it became renowned for a lack of discipline and even outright disloyalty to the Islamic government.

On the contrary, very little is known about the operations of the 83rd TFS, except that in 1985 this unit was forward deployed to TFB.6 in order to ease the burden of making lengthy transit flights from TFB.8 to CAP stations over Kharg Island. With a shorter response time, the existing CAP doctrine could now be scrapped in favour of a more efficient quick-response scramble system, with Bushehr located only 56km away from Kharg. This unit, however, stayed at TFB.6 for much longer than anticipated, and was later re-designated as the 63rd TFS.

In 1984 a number of pilots and technical officers from the 82nd TFS launched Project Sky Hawk, which involved integrating four of their F-14s with the MIM-23B I-HAWK SAM, to serve as an air-to-air missile. Reportedly initially undertaken with some help from Israel, Sky Hawk did not prove particularly successful early on, mainly due to problems that could not be solved given the limited time afforded to the project personnel. Nevertheless, the project was re-launched following the end of the war, and subsequently resulted in the development of the AIM-23C Sedjil air-to-air missile.

In 1985 and 1986, some of the most experienced pilots from the three F-14 squadrons based at TFB.8 became involved in a project to re-qualify a number of other IRIAF fliers on the Tomcat, and then participated in the establishment of the IRIAF Academy and associated training units.

During 1986, Tomcat crews at Esfahan began adapting their fighters for the carriage of general-purpose bombs. Although the Iranian F-14s subsequently flew a number of air-to-ground sorties against Iraq, such missions remained of secondary priority, since the type continued to prove vital in the air defence role.

Following the end of the war with Iraq, the IRIAF launched a major effort to return as many Tomcats to operational status as possible. With the help of a wide network of arms brokers and middlemen, increasing quantities of spare parts were acquired from various sources. Nevertheless, the stock of spares for avionics systems was never sufficient, and a large part of the fleet had to soldier on without operational radars. At the same time, many of the experienced flight crews entered early retirement after fighting a long war. Despite continuing efforts, by 2002 the condition of the remaining crews and aircraft of the 63rd TFS was so poor that the IRIAF had to withdraw it from TFB.6 and disband the unit.

Four years later, in the face of the US-led invasion of Iraq and increasing tensions with Israel, Iran finally found the will, the technical resources and the funding to revitalise the entire Tomcat fleet. In the light of the F-14's retirement from service with the US Navy, Iran was again able to clandestinely obtain considerable amounts of spares from the US. At the same time, with the help of various domestic defence companies, and primarily IACI, the air force also launched production of some critical F-14 spare parts and subsystems. Between 2006 and 2009, these efforts resulted in a large number of F-14s undergoing extensive overhauls – in some cases outright 're-building processes' – which dramatically increased the number of operational airframes.

At the time of writing there were again three fully equipped units operating the Tomcat, comprising the 81st, 82nd and 83rd TFS based at TFB.8. The latter unit usually has at least two F-14s forward deployed at TFB.6. Nevertheless, due to the continuing lack of specific avionics components, the fleet of more than 40 remaining aircraft is divided into two categories: 'parvāzi', meaning 'airworthy' but with no operational AN/AWG-9 radars and weapons systems; and 'amaliyāti', meaning 'fully mission capable', most of which have operational avionics and are considered capable of undertaking all types of air defence missions. While two examples from the latter category are usually kept on alert status at TFB.8, the former aircraft are used for training of new pilots as well as for proficiency training, and have a secondary role as fighter-bombers equipped with general-purpose bombs and AIM-9 Sidewinder air-to-air missiles in the case of a war.

84th Training Squadron

In addition to basing its F-14s at TFB.8, and making plans for reinforcing the type through the addition of F-16s, the IIAF also planned to expand the base into a major training centre towards the end of the 1980s. This project was considered particularly important since through the 1970s most Iranian pilots were trained abroad, and the air force had a severe shortage of training facilities that would satisfy its requirements. However, all corresponding plans had to be cancelled due to the Revolution of 1979. Instead, all training was subsequently stopped, leaving the air force with a large number of pilot cadets in their early years of qualification. Due to the Iraqi invasion, in the following years the IRIAF was primarily concerned with fighting a war. Only once the situation on the front lines began to stabilise did it find time to re-start recruitment and the training of new aircrews and technical personnel.

The first problem the air force faced was finding suitable equipment. Back in 1973, Iran purchased 10 Beech F33As and up to 25 F33C Bonanzas. Intended for use as primary trainers and for liaison, most of them were still in a disassembled condition as of 1983. While launching an effort to assemble and make operational the F33s within the context of Project Parastoo, the IRIAF simultaneously established contacts with Pilatus Aircraft Ltd in Switzerland, and ordered 74 PC-7 advanced turboprop twin-seat trainers. Only 35 of these had been delivered by August 1984, when US pressure led to a cancellation of the contract. The Swiss, therefore, did not deliver many technical and operational manuals, which the disappointed Iranians had to produce from scratch.

Later during the war the IRGC Ministry's Shahid Sani'ipour Aviation Complex in Esfahan launched a project to reverse-engineer the PC-7 under the local designation S.68 (S for Sepāh, meaning Islamic Revolutionary Guards, and 68 for 1368, the Persian year in which the project was completed). The project was later moved to Hessa, after the IRGC and defence ministries were merged. The only difference between the S.68 and the Swiss-made original is the Iranian aircraft's lack of British-made Martin-Baker Mk 10 ejection seats – in this respect they are similar to the last 12 PC-7s delivered directly from Switzerland. Later, the IRIAF adapted most of its PC-7s and S.68s for the carriage of gun and rocket pods, for training purposes.

Meanwhile, in 1985, the entire PC-7 fleet (followed by all the S.68s) entered service with the 84th Training Squadron, which forms the centrepiece of the IRIAF's Air Force Academy at TFB.8.

85th Advanced and Weapons Training Squadron

In the course of establishing its Air Force Academy, in 1985 the IRIAF overhauled 10 T-33As and returned them to service. The T-33As were originally delivered to the IIAF in 1956, followed by RT-33As, the latter that served with the 101st (later 11th) TRS until 1968. On their re-entry to service, the aircraft were delivered to a newly established unit, the 85th Advanced and Weapons Training Squadron, assigned to the Air Force Academy at TFB.8. In the same year, 10 F-5Bs operational with the 43rd TFS, and several F-5s purchased from Ethiopia, were also assigned to the 85th.

Following a spate of fatal accidents involving T-33s, the unit was more than relieved to be reinforced through the addition of seven FT-7s purchased from China, in 1990. The remaining T-33s were subsequently withdrawn from service, and the unit became responsible not only for training pilots on fast jets, but also for qualifying them to employ weapons.

During the 1990s the 85th Advanced and Weapons Training Squadron was reinforced again, this time through the introduction to service of the Simorgh. The Simorgh is a conversion of several available F-5A and RF-5A airframes into two-seat F-5B configuration by Hessa at Shahin-Shahr, with the help of Pakistani engineers. In addition, several F-5B airframes were overhauled, among them a number of former mounts of the 71st TFS.

Ever since, prospective IRIAF pilots receive their initial training on PC-7s of the 84th Training Squadron, after which they are divided – depending on theirs cores – into two groups. One group is then trained to fly F-5Bs and Simorghs and continues to serve on US-made fast jets, while the other is subsequently trained on FT-7s and continues in the cockpits of F-7s, MiG-29s and Su-24MKs.

TFB.8 Baba'i

To the amazement of many Western observers, and in the face of immense problems and increasing costs, the IRIAF has made the issue of retaining its unique fleet of F-14A Tomcat interceptors in service a matter of national pride. The type therefore still forms the backbone of the country's air defences.
(IRIAF)

F-14A 3-6042 is one of the fully operational Tomcats serving with the 82nd TFS. It was photographed following its complex overhaul at IACI in 2009.
(Babak Taghvaee) ▶

115

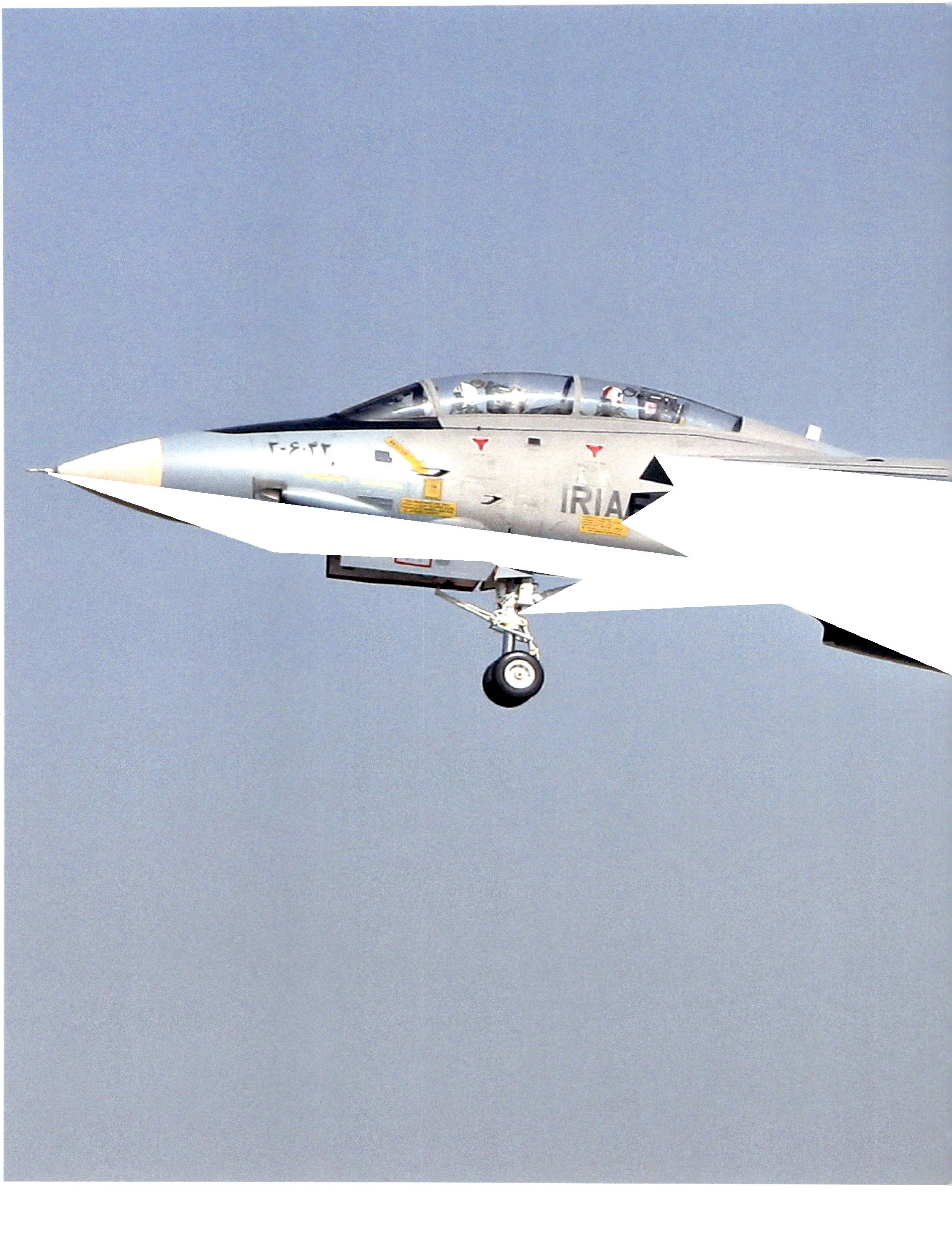
۳-۶۰۴۳
IRIAF

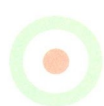

TFB.8 Baba'i

IRIAF 2010

F-14A 3-6067 was one of the last Iranian Tomcats to retain the old camouflage pattern. It was photographed at Mehrabad AB prior to a complex overhaul at IACI.
(Liam F. Devlin)

F-14A 3-6062 is currently assigned to the 83rd TFS, a unit re-established when an increasing number of Tomcats was returned to operational status though the intensive efforts of the IRIAF and IACI.
(Babak Taghvaee)

TFB.8 Baba'i

A close-up study of the forward fuselage of F-14A 3-6062, showing details of its armament to advantage. Assigned to the 83rd TFS, the aircraft is usually kept ready to scramble at the TFB.8 alert facility. The same squadron still regularly deploys pairs of Tomcats to TFB.6 in order to bolster local air defences. (Babak Taghvaee)

Details of the 'tunnel' between the engine nacelles of F-14A 3-6062, showing two AIM-7E-4 Sparrows mounted inside their bays on the lower fuselage. (Babak Taghvaee)

F-14A 3-6024 was the second F-14A to undergo a complex overhaul at IACI and receive the new camouflage pattern. The latter was tested on F-14A 3-6022 during the mid-1990s, but became a fleet-wide standard only in the last five years.
(Liam F. Devlin)

TFB.8 Baba'i

F-14A 3-6041 belonged to the first batch of F-14As to undergo complex overhaul at IACI after the IRIAF received the funding to revitalise its Tomcat fleet. Ever since, the aircraft has been assigned to the 81st TFS.
(Liam F. Devlin)

IRIAF 2010

Assigned to the 81st TFS, F-14A 3-6005 is one of the 'parvāzi' Tomcats – IRIAF F-14s that lack operational weapons systems. They are mainly used for continuation training purposes and aerial gunnery or for flying bombing missions.
(Babak Taghvaee)

TFB.8 Baba'i

Starboard view of F-14A 3-6024, together with an ATM-54A Phoenix training round. This is one of a number of Tomcats in Iranian service with a very rich combat history. It not only shot down at least six Iraqi fighters, but also participated in the famous 'Foxbat Scare' – the interception of a Soviet MiG-25R over the Caspian Sea in 1978. (Liam F. Devlin)

This close-up of the right side of the cockpit area of F-14A 3-6024 shows the extended in-flight refuelling probe (without doors, as on all Iranian Tomcats) and that all the maintenance stencilling is still applied in English, as on all other aircraft types in service with the IRIAF. (Liam F. Devlin)

123

3-6031 (foreground) and 3-6037 in the process of taking fuel from a Boeing 707 tanker. Both Tomcats were formerly assigned to the 63rd TFS until that unit was disbanded in 2006. They were subsequently reassigned to the 83rd TFS and 3-6037 is currently undergoing overhaul at IACI.
(IRIAF)

TFB.8 Baba'i

PC-7 7-9917 is one of the examples originally built in Switzerland, and therefore equipped with Martin-Baker Mk 10 ejection seats. It is still in service with the 84th Training Squadron.
(Liam F. Devlin)

7-9925 belonged to the second batch of PC-7s delivered to Iran from Switzerland without ejection seats. Sadly, the IRIAF is known to have lost several students and instructors as a result of being forced to operate insufficiently equipped training aircraft.
(Liam F. Devlin)

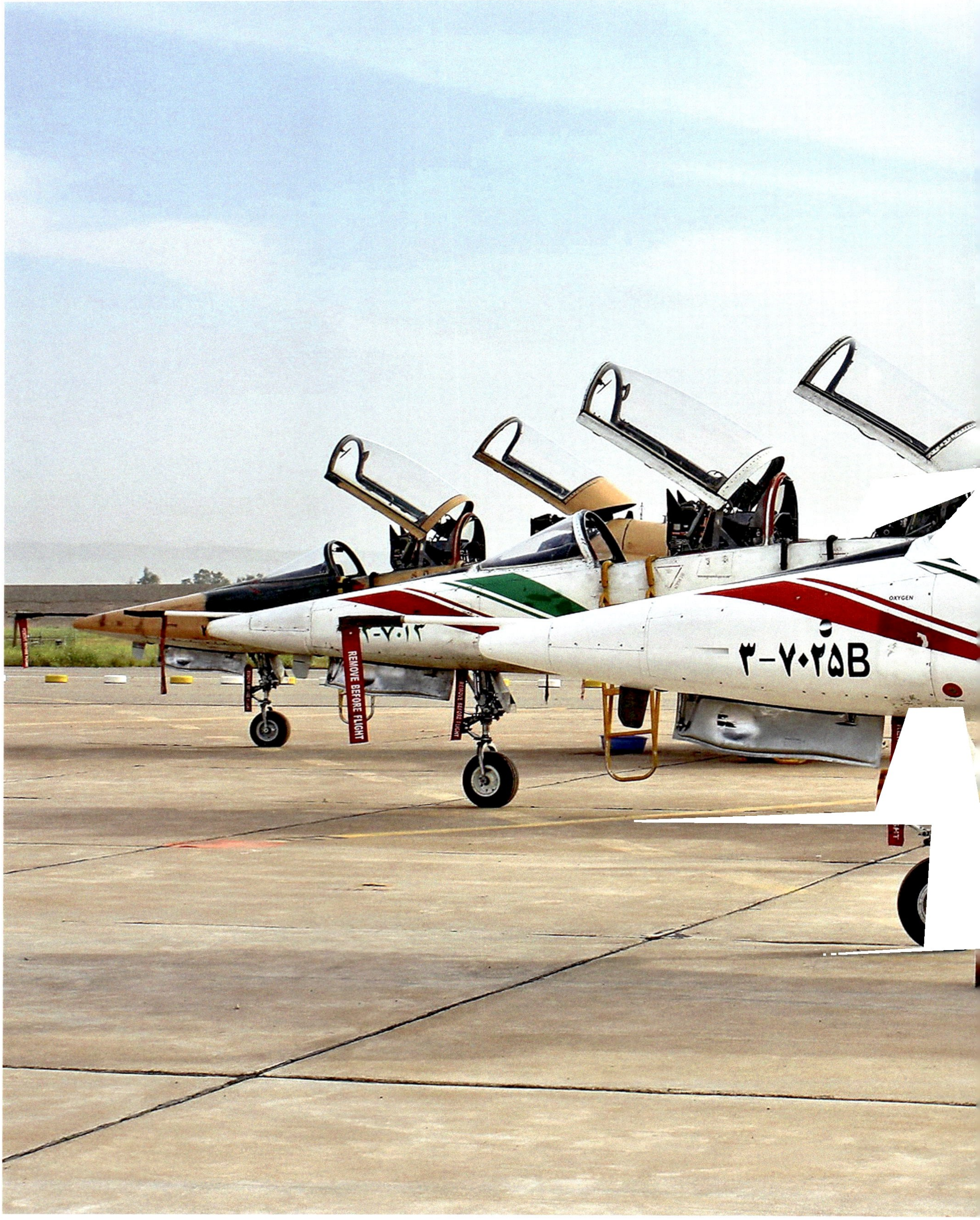
REMOVE BEFORE FLIGHT
۳-۷۰۱۲
۳-۷۰۲۵B
OXYGEN

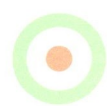

TFB.8 Baba'i

Starboard view of another F-5B Simourgh. Although all painted white overall, most of these aircraft have markings applied in different fashion. (Liam F Devlin)

A line-up including one F-5B and two F-5B Simourghs of the 85th Advanced and Weapons Training Squadron. The F-5B Simourgh in the foreground is the latest example of this type, converted from an old F-5A fuselage.
(Babak Taghvaee) ◂

TFB.8 Baba'i

F-5B 3-7012B is one of only three aircraft of the 85th Advanced and Weapons Training Squadron that retain desert camouflage. In the 1970s and the 1980s it was operated by the 43rd TFS at Vahdati AB.
(Babak Taghvaee)

These two F-5As, seen together with an F-5B Simourgh at Mehrabad AB, have a particularly interesting story to tell. Both were purchased from Ethiopia in 1984-85, together with a number of other F-5Bs, F-5Es and RF-5As, all of which participated in the Ethiopian-Somali War of 1977-78. They are still in service with the 85th Advanced and Weapons Training Squadron.
(Babak Taghvaee)

129

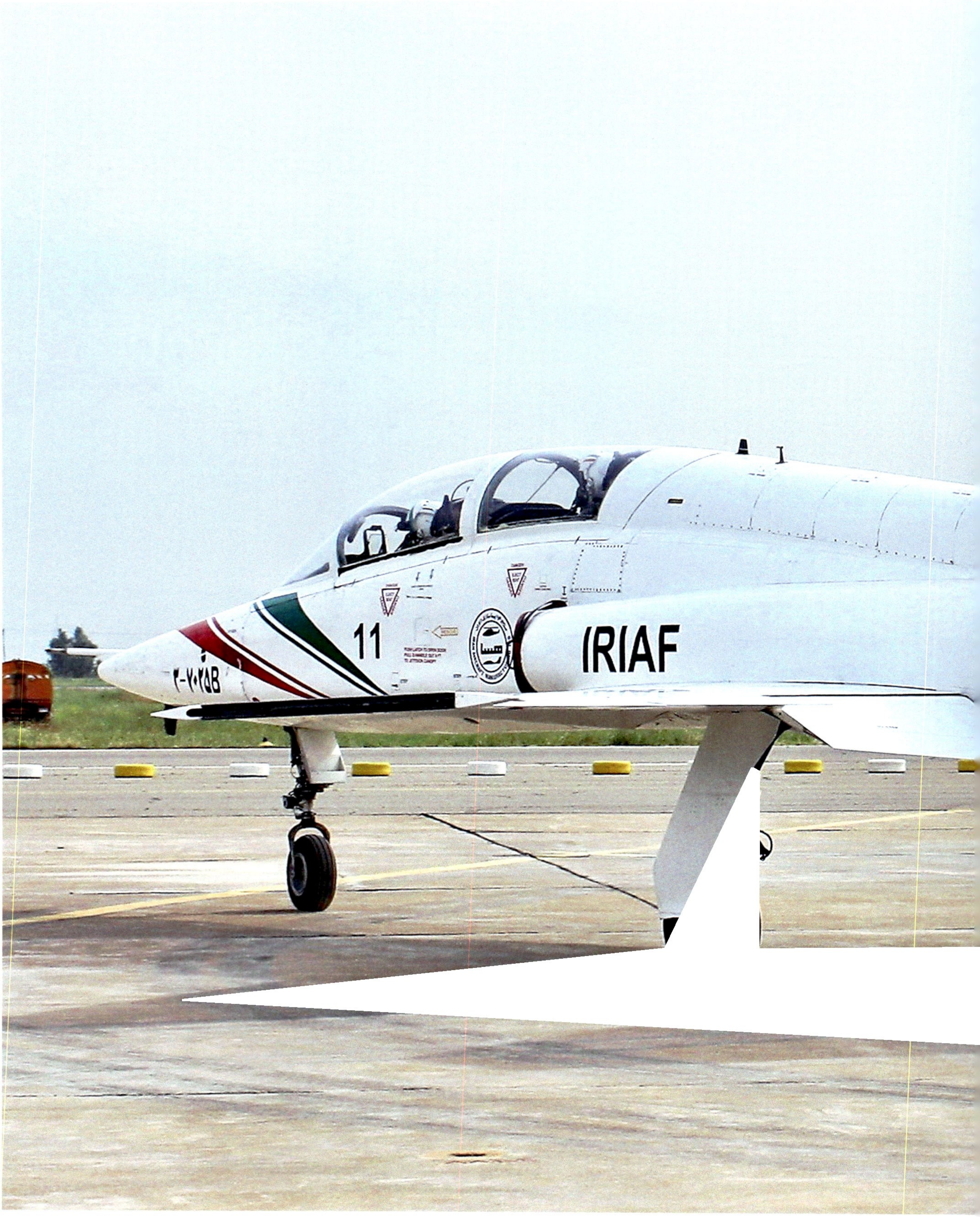
IRIAF
11

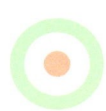

TFB.8 Baba'i

IRIAF 2010

Two F-5B Simourghs on the tarmac of TFB.4 during a public display in early 2010. The front aircraft proudly displays the emblem of the HESA company below the rear cockpit.
(Babak Taghvaee)

The F-5B Simourgh is the result of the conversion of F-5A and F-5B airframes, and its structure includes a number of locally manufactured subassemblies and components.
(Babak Taghvaee) ◄

TFB.8 Baba'i

Most FT-7Ms delivered to Iran originally wore this air superiority camouflage pattern, devised by the Chinese.
(Babak Taghvaee)

FT-7M 3-7718 was the final example to wear this attractive red and white colour scheme – prior to its overhaul in 2009.
(Babak Taghvaee)

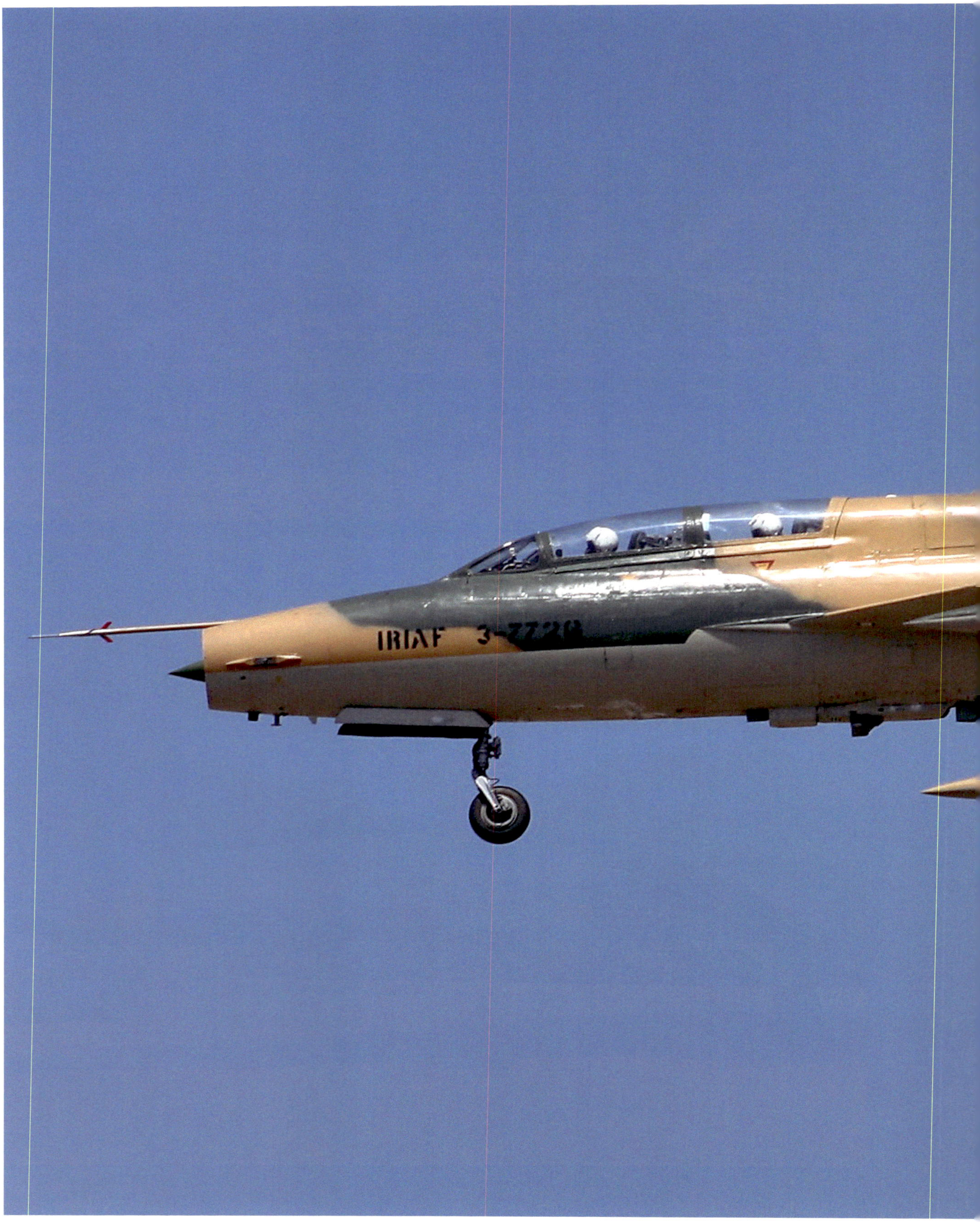
IRIAF

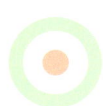

TFB.8 Baba'i

Nowadays, most IRIAF FT-7Ms have been locally overhauled and have received this camouflage pattern based on that of the F-5. This is one of only two examples in service that have been upgraded through the addition of Chinese radar warning receivers (note the antennae on top of the fin).
(Babak Taghvaee) ◄

Tactical Fighter Base 9 Bandar Abbas

Construction of a major air base near Bandar Abbas began in 1973, based on the requirement to provide the IIAF with a facility from which it could control and safeguard the strategically vital Strait of Hormuz. The first phase of construction at Bandar Abbas AB was completed in 1975, and work subsequently began to establish two F-4E units at the base: the 91st 'Sharks' and the 92nd TFS. A total of 18 hardened double aircraft shelters for Phantoms were erected in the northwest corner of the air base, with storage facilities in the northeast corner. Several batteries of MIM-23B I-HAWK SAMs protected the base, and three F-4Es armed with AIM-7Es and AIM-9s were kept on constant alert.

In the second phase of construction, the now 9th Tactical Fighter/Maritime Base (TFMB.9) was expanded by adding the facilities required to operate P-3F Orions, and in 1977, the 91st ASW Squadron moved to the base, followed by a small SAR Squadron equipped with four Bell 214Cs.

The third phase would have seen the stationing of two additional units equipped with F-4G 'Wild Weasels'. An order for the defence suppression variant of the Phantom II was placed in 1978, following extensive and often heated negotiations between Tehran and Washington. The units in question, the 93rd and 94th TFS, were to be housed inside an entirely new complex on the eastern side of the air base, together with associated storage facilities for their primary weapon, the Texas Instruments AGM-45 Shrike anti-radar missile. Such plans were never realised, as the F-4G/AGM-45 contract was cancelled as a result of the Revolution.

After the Iraqi invasion of Iran in September 1980, the 91st ASW Squadron moved to TFB.7, while the aircraft and crews of the 92nd TFS were reassigned to TFB.3. Only the 91st TFS, with barely 10 Phantoms, remained at the base for most of the 1980s.

The situation became even more critical in February 1988, when most of the pilots of this unit were killed in the crash of a C-130 near Bandar Abbas. The unit was subsequently disbanded and its remaining personnel, as well as its aircraft, were also relocated to TFB.3.

91st Tactical Fighter Squadron

In 1990 the IRIAF finally found an opportunity to re-establish its presence north of the Strait, when a new 91st TFS was formed at Bandar Abbas using 12 F-4Es plus personnel from the 31st and 32nd TFS. The new unit began intensive flying and very realistic training, but it has since suffered several losses due to accidents, including one F-4E that crashed in 1992, another in 1994, and one in 2002.

Nowadays, the 91st TFS remains the only major IRIAF unit based at TFB.9, while the 'Shark tradition' has meanwhile been appropriated more visibly by the 61st TFS (apparently using the reasoning that the waters off Bushehr contain more sharks than those further south).

The air force has also established an overhaul facility at Bandar Abbas, this being capable of completing tasks similar to those undertaken at facilities in Tehran or Bushehr.

IRIAF 2010

TFB.9 Bandar Abbas

IRIAF 2010

After almost 20 years spent in mothballs due to heavy damage sustained to the nose section, F-4E 3-6664 was rebuilt and overhauled by IACI in late 2009. It has been assigned to the 91st TFS ever since. Equipped with the TISEO TV camera system, it is one of the so-called 'Invader Phantoms', optimised for offensive operations. (Babak Taghvaee)

3-6530 is one of the F-4Es recently assigned to the re-established 91st TFS, following its overhaul by IACI at Mehrabad AB. Notable is the travel pod in Iranian national colours under the port inboard pylon, carried whenever the aircraft is deployed away from base. (Babak Taghvaee)

Tactical Fighter Base 10   Konarak

The site for the future TFB.10 was selected in the mid-1970s. Located in the middle of an extensive flat desert in southeast Iran, the facility is near the port town of Chabahar on the coast of the Gulf of Oman. The IIAF had ambitious plans to create a joint airfield and naval 'super base', where it intended to base three F-16 squadrons and construct no less than 60 hardened double aircraft shelters (including some underground) and eight shelters for alert fighters. These were to be supported by command, administrative, maintenance, and storage facilities, most of which would be constructed underground.

Construction work began in 1977, with the intention of completing the first phase by 1980, and having the entire complex ready a year later. However, in a rush to train as many new F-16 pilots as possible, but also to establish an early presence in this part of the world, the IIAF began basing some of its units at the unfinished Chabahar/Konarak AB by late 1977. As a result, the personnel had to live in provisional housing and under primitive conditions. However, the IIAF tried to keep morale high by providing frequent direct flights to Tehran and Shiraz. The 43rd TFS regularly deployed a number of F-5Bs and F-5Fs to Chabahar/Konarak, in order to train future F-16 pilots, and possibly some of the F-5E/F units later assigned to TFB.5 also came into being at TFB.10 during this period.

The Revolution put an end to all such plans and left Chabahar/Konarak AB unfinished and with an uncertain fate. Only 12 hardened aircraft shelters were complete, together with four alert shelters, and none of the underground facilities were finished. Training of new personnel was stopped and all airmen and aircraft returned to TFB.4. In addition, some elements within the Revolutionary government hotly debated the fundamental necessity of building such an expensive air and naval base at a time when Iran was no longer pursuing a regional hegemony.

101st Tactical Fighter Squadron

The IRIAF presence at TFB.10 therefore remained minimal until the mid-1980s, when surviving F-4Ds were withdrawn from active service and reorganised into a training unit, the 101st TFS, based at Chabahar. Following the war, the IRIAF for some time contemplated deploying several F-7 and FT-7 squadrons to the base. Although four new shelters for these fighters were constructed by 1992, the plan was abandoned due to the aforementioned problems encountered in operating the Chinese aircraft. Also abandoned was another major plan for re-equipment of the IRIAF with 100 Su-24Ms from Russia, and establishment of several units flying that type at TFB.10.

At the time of writing, less than a dozen old and weary F-4Ds of the 101st TFS are the only fighters currently operated from Chabahar. The aircraft were completely overhauled in the late 1990s, and a few even received modified electronics. However, the condition of these Phantoms began to deteriorate in recent years. Pilots were able to fly only one sortie a week, after which the ground personnel had to work up to 40 or more hours to prepare the aircraft for the next sortie. In 2007 the squadron suffered a loss when an F-4D crashed during a training sortie over the Gulf of Oman, killing the crew.

In 2009, Phantoms of the 101st TFS began to arrive at Mehrabad for a major overhaul. IACI also returned to service a number of stored aircraft that had sustained heavy wartime damage. Nevertheless, there is little doubt that the days of the F-4D in Iran are numbered, and if it were not for the dedication of the Chabahar crews, the type would have long been withdrawn from service.

F-4D 3-6700 on finals to TFB.10. The F-4Ds are the oldest Phantoms in service with the IRIAF, most of them having accumulated over 40 years of very intensive flying operations.
(Babak Taghvaee)

In September 2009, F-4D 3-6713 made a rare visit to TFB.1, in order to participate in the military parade over Tehran. The aircraft is seen during final checks before taking off.
(Babak Taghvaee)

TFB.10 Konarak

Thanks to the patience and great care of their maintenance crews, as well as the extensive works undertaken by IACI at Mehrabad, IRIAF F-4Ds remain in a reasonably good condition.
(Babak Taghvaee)

3-6705 rolls back to its HAS following a training sortie in the course of an IRIAF exercise. (Babak Taghvaee)

Tactical Fighter Base 14 Imam Reza

Although routinely used by the IIAF since the 1930s, this facility was not expanded into a significant air base until more recent times. In the interim, the base was used by the IRIAF during the Soviet invasion of Afghanistan and notably as a 'refuge base' during the Iran-Iraq War. At this time the airfield was known as Mashhad, although it was also briefly known as Dr Shari'ati AB after the Revolution.

Between 26 and 28 January 1991, during Operation Desert Storm, 24 Iraqi Mirage F.1EQ fighter-bombers and F.1BQ conversion trainers sought refuge in Iran. Although having an agreement with Baghdad to return such aircraft after the end of the conflict, Iran subsequently decided to keep them as part of their war reparations, which Iraq otherwise refused to pay. After their arrival, all the Mirages were initially concentrated at TFB.3, where they were stored in the open. In 1993, however, Col Naghdi-Beik, an inspired F-4 pilot and commander, made a test flight with the type. Although lacking any technical documentation or previous training on the Mirage, he was very satisfied and his enthusiastic report gave the IRIAF the idea to return all 24 Mirages to service.

In the same year, a significant quantity of spare parts was acquired from Libya, as well as from various other sources, and in 1994 the IRIAF also received some help from Pakistani technicians. Initially, six Mirage F.1s were overhauled by IACI at Mehrabad, while work on the other aircraft was subsequently undertaken on site at TFB.3. Later the same year, while additional IRIAF personnel were trained on the type, Col Naghdi-Beik flew the first nine Mirages to Mashhad AB, which was subsequently officially renamed as the Imam Reza 14th Tactical Fighter Base (TFB.14).

The next problem that had to be solved was that of local facilities. Even as of 1994, the IRIAF only had one ramp in the northeast corner of the airfield. Although capable of supporting operations by the largest aircraft in the inventory, the base was insufficient for operating even a single permanently based fighter-bomber squadron, and the new TFB.14 lacked appropriate housing and administrative facilities, storage depots and aircraft shelters.

141st and 142nd Tactical Fighter Squadrons

The IRIAF had very few spare parts and weapons for its Mirages, and they thus proved of minimal value. Despite this, Col Naghdi-Beik pressed on, and by 1995 two newly established units had become operational at the 'new' air base: the 141st and 142nd TFS. Construction of facilities at Mashhad proceeded very slowly, however, and by 2000 only a single maintenance hangar and two hardened aircraft shelters had been erected. The limited progress certainly hampered groundcrews' efforts to keep their new mounts in an operational condition. Construction of four additional shelters, and a taxiway to the runway, was only completed in 2009.

In the following years, the Mirages flew frequent training and reconnaissance sorties along the eastern borders of Iran, and eventually saw some combat service in support of border security and anti-insurgency operations. These operations were conducted in the course of a major campaign against drug-trafficking bands from Afghanistan and Pakistan.

By 2000, most of the Mirages required overhaul, and Iran opened secret negotiations with France, attempting to acquire spares as well as weapons. However, although the French were initially enthusiastic, making offers of up to 140 second-hand Mirage F.1s as well as 1,000 air-to-air missiles, further talks were cancelled after pressures from the US. The IRIAF thus had to satisfy itself with putting a handful of Mirages through overhaul at IACI. In the course of this work they received a new 'air superiority' camouflage pattern, similar to that now used on the F-14s.

In August 2001 a 141st TFS Mirage F.1BQ was engaged by an SA-14 Gremlin MANPADS fired by Taliban forces while on a reconnaissance sortie along the Afghan border. The crew, consisting of the TFB.14's commanding officer, Gen Nasser Habibi, and a much younger co-pilot, managed to keep the badly damaged aircraft airborne for some time while attempting to fly back to their base. However, the engine failed on the approach. While the crew attempted to turn the aircraft away from residential areas, the Mirage stalled and crashed, killing both pilots.

Following this incident, the IRIAF stored most of its Mirages and disbanded the 142nd TFS. The 141st TFS continued operations on a small-scale basis until 2003, but had to be reinforced by five F-5Es from the 21st TFS in reaction to the escalating situation in Afghanistan.

Eventually, the 141st TFS ceased all Mirage operations, and by 2004 all the aircraft of this type were stored in the open at Mashhad. Instead, this squadron is now flying a small number of F-5Es, and from time to time has to be reinforced through temporary deployments of other fighter units. A pair of F-5s is usually kept on alert. Only three Mirage F.1BQs and three Mirage F.1EQs are occasionally flown, mainly on ceremonial occasions, such as parades in Tehran.

TFB.14 Imam Reza

3-6215 is one of the former Iraqi Mirage F.1EQ-6s operated by the IRIAF in the 1990s and now stored at TFB.14. Since it had a few flying hours left since its last periodic overhaul, it was taken out of mothballs and flown to Tehran to participate in the parade on 22 September 2009.
(Babak Taghvaee)

Although it received a partial fresh coat of paint, Mirage F.1BQ 3-6407 also had to be pulled out of storage for participation in the Holy Defence Week Parade in September 2009.
(Babak Taghvaee)

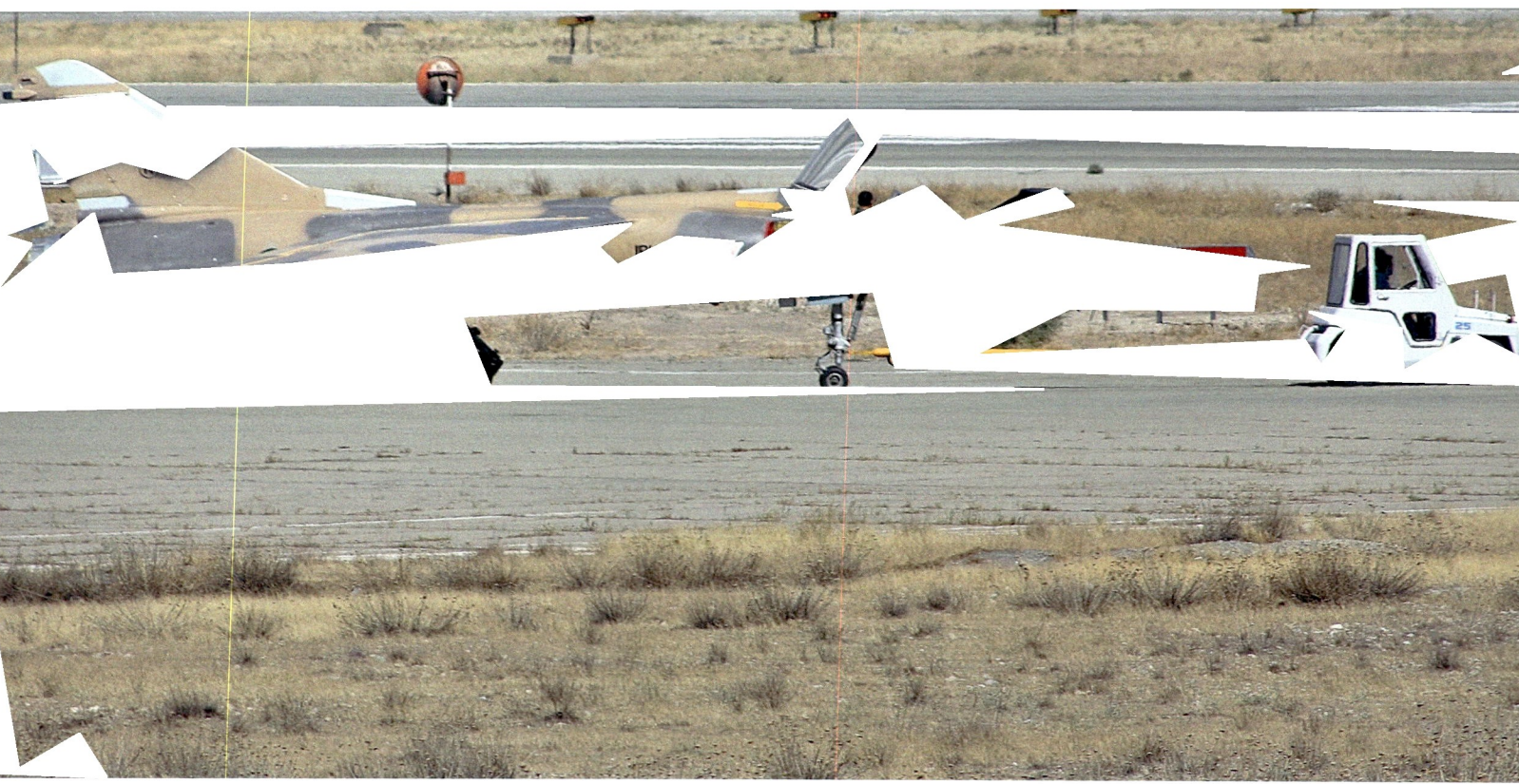

3-6213 is towed away after landing at Mehrabad. Although Iran and France held some talks concerning the possible overhaul and upgrade of the fleet, around 10 years ago, no agreement was reached, in turn sealing the fate of all the Iranian Mirages.
(Babak Taghvaee)

Other IRIAF bases

Birjand

Constructed in the 1970s, Birjand airfield, some 150km from the Afghan border, is primarily a civilian facility, although the IIAF had considered deployment of its combat aircraft there in case of emergency. In the early 1990s the IRIAF developed a plan to turn Birjand airfield into a major air base. Although Birjand was already assigned the official designation of Tactical Fighter Base 13 such plans were never realised and no construction work was ever undertaken.

Dowshan Tappeh

Sometimes known as the TFB.11, and still serving as the main headquarters of the IRIAF, no units are permanently assigned to the former Dowshan Tappeh AB. However, during the Iran-Iraq War, F27 and C-130 transports frequently landed here to offload badly wounded soldiers for treatment in the modern IRIAF hospital and other nearby medical facilities. Nowadays, the local runway is entirely surrounded by the sprawling city of Tehran. In a relatively poor condition, the runway is only used by helicopters and light liaison aircraft.

Gayem al-Mohammad

Officially declared operational in October 2007, this air base constructed some 150km west of Birjand is not known to house any IRIAF units.

Ghaleh Morghi

The oldest Iranian airfield ceased serving as a major air base in the 1960s. By the 1980s, only the air force's Basic Training Squadron, originally flying AT-6Ds and later equipped with F33As and F33Cs, remained stationed here. Following an accident in the course of which an F33C made an emergency landing on a busy main street in southern Tehran, and the crash of another F33C on a parking lot inside the city, it was decided to cease all flying from Ghaleh Morghi, and to move the IRIAF Basic Training Squadron to Koushk-e Nosrat airfield, outside Tehran. Sadly, the historic Ghaleh Morghi airfield is now destined for demolition and redevelopment by the Tehran Municipality.

Jask

Constructed in the 1970s near Jask, on the coast of the Gulf of Oman, the main purpose of this small facility was serving IIAF transport aircraft and commercial air traffic. In the early 1990s the IRIAF explored the idea of developing it into its TFB.12, and stationing most of its light transport aircraft there. Corresponding plans were abandoned mainly due to a lack of funding and interest on the part of the government.

Kish

Constructed in the 1970s, the small Kish Air Force Base has no permanently assigned flying units, but houses ground-based early warning units.

Kushk-e Nosrat

Koushk-e Nosrat airfield, situated south of Tehran near a village with the same name, was constructed by the IIAF in the 1960s, to be used in emergencies and for dispersal of aircraft based at TFB.1. During the late 1960s and 1970s, this airfield and its associated firing range frequently hosted the popular flight demonstrations by the IIAF's Golden Crown team. Following the Revolution, this airfield was used only as an emergency airstrip. By 2004 the facility was in very poor condition, but after the IRIAF decided to move its Basic Training Squadron from Ghaleh Morghi to Koushk-e Nosrat reconstruction of the runway and construction of appropriate facilities got under way. Work was mainly completed by 2005 and the airfield is now in active use by the air force.

Although painted in the same livery as the F33As operated by the Air Force Academy, some aircraft of this type are used for liaison purposes. This example is usually in service at TFB.4.
(Liam F. Devlin)

F33A 4-9640 is one of the aircraft now operated by the Basic Training Squadron at Kushk-e-Nosrat airfield. This can be recognised by the swallow emblem on the fin, or the abbreviation 'F-A', which stands for Flight Academy.
(Babak Taghvaee)

Other IRIAF bases

Following the crash of F33A 4-9609 in downtown Tehran in November 1999, during which the crew was lucky to survive with only slight injuries, the entire Bonanza fleet moved to Kushk-e Nosrat airfield.
(Babak Taghvaee)

Order of Battle

Tactical Fighter Base 1 Mehrabad

11th TFS
MiG-29

Wing patch
MiG-29

ERS
RC-130H/Boeing 707

12th TAS
C-130E/H

Wing patch
C-130E/H

Tanker & Transport Squadron
Boeing 707 and 747

Wing patch
Boeing 707

Wing patch
Boeing 747

F27 Squadron
F27

Wing patch
F27

Falcon Star Squadron
Falcon 20 and 50

VIP Transport Squadron
Airbus and Boeing

11th HTS
CH-47C

SAR Squadron
Bell 214C

IRIAF pilots wear four types of patches: 'wings' patches signifying the aircraft type on which they are qualified; other patches showing the pilot's level of qualification on a specific aircraft type (and usually based on former IIAF unit insignia); unit insignia patches (where worn); and various other 'individual' patches.

IRIAF 2010

Tactical Fighter Base 2 Tabriz

21st TFS
F-5

21st TFS
F-5 500hrs +

21st TFS
F-5 1,000hrs +

Wing patch
F-5E

23rd TFS
MiG-29

Wing patch
MiG-29

Saegheh Squadron
Saegheh

Tactical Fighter Base 3 Nojeh

31st TFS
F-4E

32nd TFS
F-4E

Aircraft patch
RF-4

Aircraft patch
F-4 up to 1,000hrs

Wing patch
F-4

Tactical Fighter Base 4 Vahdati

41st TFS
F-5E/F

42nd TFS
F-5E/F

43rd TFS
F-5B

Aircraft patch
F-5 1,000hrs +

Aircraft patch
F-5 2,000hrs +

Wing patch
F-5E

Order of Battle

Tactical Fighter Base 5 Ardestani

51st TFS
F-7N/FT-7N

52rd TFS
F-7N/FT-7N

53rd TFS
F-7N/FT-7N

Aircraft patch
F-7 500hrs +

Aircraft patch
F-7 2,000hrs +

Wing patch
F-7

Wing patch
F-7

Tactical Fighter Base 6 Yassini

61st TFS
F-4E

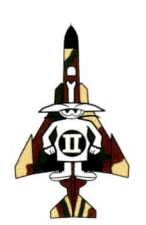

Wing patch
F-4

Tactical Fighter Base 7 Dowran

71st TFS
Su-24MK

Wing patch
Su-24

72nd TAS
C-130E/H

Wing patch
C-130E/H

155

IRIAF 2010

Wing patch	71st ASW	Liaison Squadron	SAR Squadron
Il-76	P-3F	PC-6	Bell 214C

Tactical Fighter Base 8 Baba'i

81st TFS	82nd TFS	83rd TFS	Wing patch	Aircraft informal
F-14A	F-14A	F-14A	F-14A	F-14A

84th TS	IRIAF Academy	Wing patch	85th TFS
S-68 and PC-7	S-68 and PC-7	PC-7	F-5B and FT-7

Wing patch	Aircraft patch	Aircraft patch	Wing patch
F-5B	F-5B up to 500hrs	F-5B 500hrs +	F-7

156

Order of Battle

Tactical Fighter Base 9 Bandar Abbas

91st TFS
F-4E

Wing patch
F-4

Tactical Fighter Base 10 Konarak

TFB.10

101st TFS
F-4D

Wing patch
F-4D

Tactical Fighter Base 14 Imam Reza

141st TFS
Mirage F.1

21st TFS Detachment
F-5 500hrs +

21st TFS Detachment
F-5 1,000hrs +

Wing patch
F-5E

Kushk-e Nosrat

IRIAF
Flight Academy

IRIAF
Flight Academy Center

Wing patch
F33

Map of Iran

IRANIAN AVIATION REVIEW

ISSN 2151-8122   ADVERTISE-FREE,   BY-MONTHLY MAGAZINE,   PRINTED IN USA BY TOP KIT PUBLISHING

World's most comprehensive source for past and present military and commercial aviation in Iran

- Air Force
- Army Aviation
- Naval Aviation
- Revolutionary Guard
- Airlines
- Airports and Air Bases
- Cargo Operators
- General Aviation
- Government Organizations
- Industrial Companies
- and much more...

Data, Photographs and Illustrations you will not find in any other aviation magazine

In-depth articles • Special reports • Operational data • Military serials • Civil registrations • Aircraft type review • Aviation organizations fleet
Rare, never-before-published photographs • Superb illustrations • Past and present airlines • Flashback to history • News and fleet update

for more information and ordering

www.iranianaviation.com

HARPIA PUBLISHING

Glide With Us Into The World of Aviation Literature

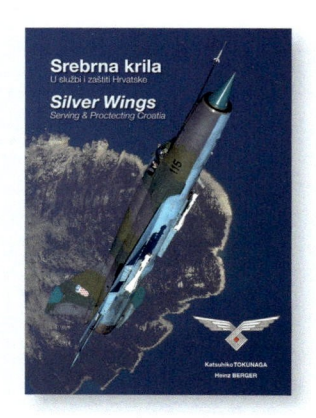

Silver Wings – Serving & Protecting Croatia
Katsuhiko Tokunaga and Heinz Berger
160 pages, 30x22 cm, hardcover with jacket
48.00 Euro   ISBN 978-0-9825539-1-6

The world-famous Japanese aviation photographer Katsuhiko Tokunaga covers the activities of today's Croatian Air Force in his well known and destinctive, nearly artistic style.
Following a brief introduction into the history of Croatian Air Force from 1991 until 2009, this exclusive, top quality photo monography provides dozens of high-quality photographs of the aircraft currently in service, and rich detail about the life, work and action of the men and women serving and protecting Croatia.
Appendices list the technical data of all aircraft in service and the current order of battle, together with all the unit insignia.

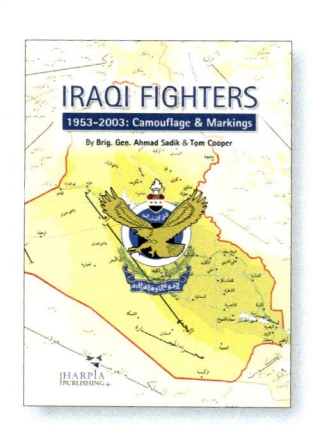

Iraqi Fighters 1953–2003 Camouflage & Markings
Brig. Gen. Ahmad Sadik and Tom Cooper
156 pages, 28x21cm, softcover
29.95 Euro   ISBN 978-0-615-21414-6

Richly illustrated with photographs and artworks, this book provides an exclusive insight into service history of 13 fighter jet types – from Vampires and Hunters to MiG-29s and Su-24s – that served with Royal Iraqi Air Force (RIrAF) and Iraqi Air Force (IrAF) between 1953 and 2003.
The result is a detailed history of RIrAF and IrAF markings, serial numbers and camouflage patterns, the in-depth history of each Iraqi fighter squadron, their equipment over the time as well as unit and various special insignias.
An appendix lists the exisiting plastic scale model kits in 1/72, 1/48 and 1/32 scale as well as decals sheets in regards to Iraqi Air Force.

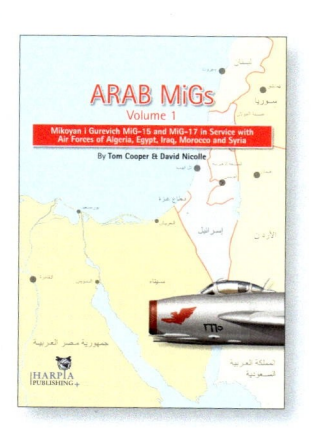

Arab MiGs Volume 1, MiG-15s and MiG-17s, 1955–1967
Tom Cooper and David Nicole
256 pages, 28x21 cm, softcover
35.95 Euro   ISBN 978-0-9825539-2-3

This study – the first in a series of similar publications – provides a unique and previously unavailable insight into the service of both types with five Arab air forces, including Algeria, Egypt, Iraq, Morocco and Syria. It tells the story of people that flew MIG-15s and MiG-17s, several of whom became dominant political figures in most recent history of these countries, and completes this with a review of combat operations in Yemen, as well as in three wars between the Arabs and the Israelis. Over 200 photos, colour artworks, maps and tables illustrate the story of the aircraft and their crews, as well as unit insignia in unprecedented detail. Extensive lists of serial- and construction numbers are provided as well.

THE AVIATION BOOKS OF A DIFFERENT KIND
UNIQUE TOPICS I **IN-DEPTH RESEARCH** I **RARE PICTURES** I **HIGH PRINTING QUALITY**

www.harpia-publishing.com